# APPLYING FOR A TEACHING JOB

*The definitive guide to writing a great application for a job as a teacher, HoD, HoY, AHT, DHT or headteacher*

## Theo Griff

DISCLAIMER: This book has been written with reasonable skill and care, and in good faith as the personal opinion of the author.

However, it gives advice or suggestions on a provisional basis that readers are free to accept or reject, using their own personal and professional judgment, with no liability being incurred by the author.

This book relates to teaching posts in England and Wales, mainly in schools but also in colleges, although many points will also be relevant elsewhere.

# CONTENTS

# SCHOOL LEADERS COMMENT ON THIS BOOK

**Primary headteacher in the North of England**: *What a fantastic book! With all of the information in one place, it is essential reading in order to make that all-important first impression count. It would make my life so much easier if every candidate read this*

**Head of Maths in Yorkshire:** *A book like this is really needed, judging by the applications we receive.*

**Secondary headteacher in the North**: *I do like this book - detailed, thorough, great advice and some nice touches of gentle humour.*

**Assistant head teacher and ITT mentor**: *Helping trainees with their applications, this was a godsend. Useful too, for my own next step!*

## Extracts from reviews of earlier editions

*This is an excellent guide for teachers looking for another post from new teachers to senior teaching posts.*

*As a recruitment specialist I recommend this is on the standard reading for all new teachers.*

*I do work as a consultant offering support and advice to trainees, young teachers and even senior teachers looking to apply for headships. This little book contains advice that all of these teachers - no matter how experienced or not - can use to help them apply for and get the next teaching post. Well written, succinct and stuffed with sage advice, tips, what to do and what not to do, the book ought to be the go-to manual for applicants.*

*Theo Griff's book is a 'must read' for anyone in the teaching profession who wishes to avail themselves of sound and well-researched advice written by an author who has significant experience in processing applications for teaching posts and in selecting those successful in moving on to the interview stage.*

*Whether you are a Beginning Teacher looking to get onto that all-important first rung of your teaching career ladder, or an aspiring Head, this pithy and practical book will help you to avoid the common pitfalls of applications.*

*There are lots of really helpful tips which enables the individual to present themselves in the best possible way. I absolutely love the way the book takes you through the application process stage by stage.*

*This is a sensible, straightforward book that gives great advice no teacher applying for a job can afford to be without. Whatever your desired next step in teaching, from NQT to headship, this book has something for you.*

*The helpful, straightforward advice contained in this book really is a great investment.*

*A really useful guide to applying for jobs that every NQT should read and every experienced teacher applying for promotion internal or external should read to remind them of the basics.*

*A brilliant book, read in conjunction with Interview for a teaching job which is equally as good. Full of good sound advice. A must read for all.*

*This book will completely change how you write your applications for the better.*

*A must read for anyone aspiring to the next level up in the career. Theo gives insightful, concise, and practical advice on how to really make you stand out from other candidates. I have 12 years of teaching experience, but this book has changed my viewpoint on making a great application.*

*Very useful book. Some brilliant nuggets of information.*

*I've been following Theo Griff for years on the TES forums and the book is in keeping with her usual firm but fair advice. It's easy to read and informative and it's made me really excited about returning to teaching. I'm looking forward to buying the next book to get all the useful advice I will need for interviews!*

This is the companion volume to **Interview for a Teaching Job**, also available in Amazon Kindle.

# INTRODUCTION

After more than 20 years in education leadership, and over a decade of supporting teachers on an online education advice forum, Theo Griff has written this book full of up-to-date tips and suggestions to help you nail that job as a teacher, a middle or a senior leader through an effective application.

This book answers many of the questions that you may be wondering about, and perhaps even some that you have never thought of.

Do you know where not to look for applications advice?

Are you ready to apply for a teaching post?

Are you aware which documents you will need to have to hand?

Who should be your referees, and which will look a daft— or fishy—choice?

How do you tell your headteacher that you are looking elsewhere?

Which level of post should you aim for?

Which would be the most appropriate type of school for you?

What makes an effective application for a faith school?

What makes an effective application for an independent

school?

When should you apply for a job?

Where do you find the teaching vacancies to apply for?

How do you research a school before applying?

Should you visit a school before applying?

Do you know the 4 main errors to avoid in an application?

Are you an internal candidate?

Is a speculative letter useful?

What are the 3 main parts of an effective application?

Is a Curriculum Vitae necessary?

Do you know how to fill in the application form?

Can you ask for referees not to be contacted just yet?

What should you put as the reason for leaving?

Supporting statement, cover letter, letter of application – which is which?

How do you produce a professional and effective letter or statement?

Why and how do you draft an executive summary?

What makes an effective application for an SLT post?

How can you apply for a teaching job from a potential position of weakness?

Can you leave a school very fast?

Is supply teaching a good basis for an application?

How can you return to teaching after being out of the classroom?

How can you return to teaching after working in a school

abroad?

How best to apply with a record of ill-health absences?

How do you get a new job after redundancy?

Can you still get a job with a settlement agreement?

Can you get a job with an agreed reference?

Can you get a job with a criminal record or a disqualification under the Childcare Act?

# 1. BEFORE YOU START

# WHERE NOT TO LOOK FOR APPLICATIONS ADVICE

D o take care where you look for support in preparing an application. Internet sites are often of little use, because they are business not school-orientated (I cite in particular Forbes.com as somewhere to avoid when preparing either an application or an interview), or because they are American. You must avoid producing an application that looks as though you are applying for a job in Dallas with Exxon.

Using non-specialist advisors on applications – by which I mean those not specialising in education appointments – can also be a poor decision. This letter is not a model for an application for a teaching post.

# AN EXAMPLE LETTER NOT TO COPY

*Dear Mr Brown*

*I am replying to your advertisement for a supply teacher vacancy. After reading the job description I feel very confident that I have all the experience and abilities that you are looking for.*

*I currently work very near to Brownlee High School and I feel that a move to your school would suit me perfectly as not only do I have the required skill sets, but I am also familiar to the area and the local community. I am aware of the high reputation a award winning school like Brownlee has within the city and am keen to be associated with such a well respected educational institution.*

*I feel that one of my greatest strengths as a teacher is the ability to meet each students unique needs by having an in-depth understanding of their abilities and needs. My experiences include tutoring, organizing daily activities, and keeping students organised and controlled, all requirements asked for in the job advert.*

*I feel Brownlee High School can benefit from my four years of teaching experience and my ability to educate young minds and help them to develop into responsible successful individuals.*

*I hope that you will consider my application and I would welcome a phone call so that we might be able to set up an interview. If you need any further information then please do not hesitate to contact me. I thank you for your time and I look forward to hearing from you.*

*Yours sincerely*

Once you have read this book and learned what to do – and what not to do – in an application for a teaching post, come back and look at this letter again. Can you identify at least 12 inappropriate things about it? Answers at the end of the book.

I have also seen senior leadership applications, unsuccessful applications, that have been prepared by paying several hundred pounds to an agency specialising in helping people get jobs. Non-specialist agencies, who produce applications full of waffle and trite sentences. Do not waste your money on these.

Finally, if you are a NQT, do be a little cautious in accepting blindly the advice of your university tutors, as although they are very well-meaning and wish to support you, they normally do not have experience of appointing teachers to positions in schools. Your school-based mentor, however, is probably a head of department and does have this experience, so their advice is often very helpful. Recently, one university tutor told PGCE students that all application letters should be handwritten. No, they should not. This is not the Middle Ages; headteachers need to know that you are able to write effectively using modern technology, as you will be required to do in your teaching career.

So where should you get your advice? From this book, and from other people like me who have very many years of experience of appointing teachers to a wide range of educational establishments, have read thousands of application forms and supporting statements, and have conducted hundreds of interviews.

I shall sometimes briefly repeat information at different points in the book so that you have all the right advice to hand when reading any particular section.

# 2. GETTING READY TO APPLY FOR A TEACHING POST

There is groundwork to be done before you sit down to apply for any post. Spending a weekend – yes, it might take that long – gathering and organising this information will make any application much easier, because you will have everything at your fingertips, ready to slot it into the application form.

# HOW TO ORGANISE YOUR FILES

F irst you need to **organise your computer files**. Start a whole new folder on your computer and call it *Applications*. Inside this folder set up a folder for all your information as I suggest below, plus a separate sub-folder under *Current applications* for each school that you apply to, with its name. When you download documents from the school website, or are sent them by the school secretary, put them in this school's folder, even if they are PDF documents and the rest of the documents are Word.

Any documents that you have to fill in and return to the school, change the original name immediately to include the school name and your name, as well as what they are. You can have very long filenames with a lot of information – I have just tested *ApplicationFormPhysicsTeacher HighviewSchoolTheodoreGriffiths.* You don't need it that long, and if you do have very long filenames, it can sometimes cause problems when copying files and folders, so I do not recommend it. However, you could put *AppFormPhysicsHighviewTGriffiths,* although that is probably a little over-long too. It is essential that you do rename this file from the school, as the following tale will illustrate.

Once when I was running a course for teachers on applying for a post, one person there told us that she contacted a school about a vacancy, and was e-mailed details of the post, and an application form. When she opened the form to start filling it in, she discovered that it was already filled in by another candidate for the same post. That teacher had received from the school a file called *Application Form*, had saved it like that, filled it in and sent it back to the school, who had downloaded it and saved it, thereby overwriting their blank form. They then sent it out to subsequent candidates. A cautionary tale.

Next, consider whether you need stationery to help you organise the physical files, that is everything that cannot be stored – and backed up – on the computer. I suggest that you choose a ring binder with separators, or some A4 plastic envelope files – the ones with a press-stud fastening - as your physical files. You will need them for any documents where you need to have originals to show schools. Anything else goes on the computer as suggested above.

# THE DOCUMENTS YOU WILL NEED TO HAVE TO HAND

The following are what you are going to need to have to hand when applying, so get them set up either on the computer or in physical files.

1. Qualifications
2. Professional appointments
3. Professional development
4. Performance management
5. Pupil outcomes
6. Trumpet file (yes, really)
7. Current applications

If you are a NQT, you will not have 2 to 5. Don't worry – that is only to be expected.

The **Qualifications folder on the computer** will have one document with all your qualifications set out, with date and details – grade, exam board, name of school, college, university. In a physical file, you will also hold originals of the certificates. If you don't have your GCSE and A-level certificates (have you thought of asking your parents if they have them somewhere at home?) it won't matter all that much in most cases, but you will certainly need to have the originals of your degree(s) and QTS. If you don't have these, then you need now to contact the university and enquire how to get a replacement, as it is quite common for schools to ask you to bring them to interview, along with formal ID. Some schools do ask for your A-level certificates, so if you can possibly get them, do so.

I suggest that to this computer document of qualifications you also add your national insurance (NI) number and your teacher reference number (TRN), so that you have all this information to hand when needed. Some old application forms call the TRN the DfE or the DFES number, by the way. It is found on your QTS certificate, and looks something like this: 14/12345, with 2014 being the year that you gained QTS. It can often also be found on your payslip, if you are a serving teacher. You can contact Capita to get it as it is also used for your pension details; alternatively contact the DfE on qts.enquiries@education.gov.uk or 0207 593 5394. Do all this now if you don't have your QTS certificate and the number, so you are prepared for applications.

Your **Professional Appointments folder on the computer** will have a document of one or possibly two pages with all your teaching appointments set out; if you have also had other school roles, such as teaching assistant, include those too. Put them in chronological order, earliest first, and ensure that you have full details of each of these posts:

**Dates**, and check that you get these right – a school appointment normally runs from September to August, with the next post beginning straight afterwards; don't accidentally leave gaps.

**Name, address and type of school**, possibly also NOR – Number on Roll, i.e. how many pupils. This is sometimes required on application forms.

**Official title** of your position.

**Salary on leaving**. I do hope that you are not going to tell me that you have no idea! You should have been keeping all your payslips neatly together with treasury tags from the very start. If you haven't been doing this, then start now and continue until you retire, keeping them all. If there is ever any dispute about your pension contributions, you will want to have this proof of payment. For your current post you will, of course, have your current salary. I suggest that you don't put this salary in the file as during your applications season it might increase, and it would be daft to put the former salary in by mistake, just because you took it from here.

**Additional separate pages for each position** On these you will put a brief note of what your role actually was, and any outcomes or achievements. I suggest separate pages here for most of your jobs, although you can best decide on this, because it is helpful to look at a whole page to get an overall picture. Do remember to add details later on when you suddenly remember something that you achieved or contributed. Try putting a heading saying: *I had specific responsibility for* and another saying: *The results of my contributions included* and see what you can put under these headings. You may well surprise yourself!

Your **Professional Development folder on the computer** will list all the courses that you have attended, with dates and, if you have a record of this, the provider. Many people think that professional development just means *I went on a course*. But professional development means a lot more than that.

What happened at the beginning of the year in September? Didn't you attend sessions on Child Protection, Safeguarding and Prevent? Most schools do that then, and that is professional development. What about other in-house training that has been done at school? Can you remember what was done on your training days last year? Have you done any shadowing of colleagues, paired observations or learning walks?

Another source of CPD that people often forget is the weekly or fortnightly staff meetings, which may have a short item on useful teaching and learning tips. You might also have these in your department or Key Stage meetings too. All these are professional development, as is formal sharing and feedback from colleagues who have been able to go on a course.

Now you are not going to list all of those in-house development opportunities with dates. But at the very least, jot down in this file every so often the subject of all these types of session. Then when you are filling out an application, just include a sentence on the application form along these lines: *Regular attendance at in-school training sessions on subjects such as X, Y and Z.*

The **Performance Management folder** (it may be called Appraisal in your school) will have a document with dates and brief summaries of your objectives each year and the outcomes. Remember also to include any positive comments that were made by your appraiser (*In the recent appraisal cycle my classroom management was noted by the AHT as being particularly effective in supporting progress of all pupils*) and the same for your classroom observations. You are gathering here evidence that could be dropped into an application letter, and this is a document that you will be constantly updating and adding to.

Your **Pupil Outcomes folder** contains examination results for your classes, both raw and value-added. Jot down also how they compare with other groups or other subjects. If you teach A-level, how many went on to study your subject at University? The outcomes may not be examinations, of course, but progression in other spheres.

Anything measurable and anything comparable (*In a GCSE cohort where the average attainment was X, my group achieved Y*), get it down in writing while you remember it, because you may want to use it later. You will update this every summer after the results days. Don't forget that internal data is also useful, especially if you don't have examination groups; this will be particularly important for most years in primary, and KS3.

The **Trumpet file will probably be a physical file** (unless you scan everything in); it is where you blow your own trumpet. Even a NQT can have one of these. You keep here all the letters from parents, the thank-you cards from pupils, you jot down any compliment you receive from a colleague.

When I was a headteacher, I used to write regularly to staff to thank them, to praise them or to pass on a compliment that someone had made to me about them; one colleague being interviewed for a promotion produced a Trumpet file with 18 of these letters from me as evidence of the value of her contributions to the school. So jot them down all the time, whenever a colleague says something that makes you feel good.

The role of the Trumpet file is dual. Occasionally you can make a brief passing reference to it in an application or an interview (*The effectiveness of my role as Head of Year was shown when I received a large number of letters from parents thanking me for my actions*). But above all the Trumpet file is for you to read when things have not gone too well in school, or when you have had another unsuccessful application. You use it to console yourself, to help you realise that you do, indeed, have a great deal to offer to a school.

Even a NQT can have a Trumpet file – some positive comments from your University Tutor as well as from your school mentor or colleagues would go in here.

Your **Current Applications folder** is self-explanatory. You will of course have separate sub-folders for each school and its application. Keep there the Person Specification and Job Description that you have downloaded; if you are less comfortable with on-screen working, you may consider printing them off so that you can highlight points. You will store here the details about the school, and your various drafts, and finally the completed versions of the application form, the letter of application and the executive summary (Don't know what that is? It will be explained later).

In this folder you should also keep a document with the names and full contact details of your referees. Get their names and titles correct, include professional address at school, phone numbers, e-mails, fax, if they still use this.

# 3. THE PROFESSIONAL APPROACH TO AN APPLICATION

T his is the moment to ensure that everything about your application is thoroughly professional. You will of course be ensuring that you are honest and truthful, but let's look at other aspects.

# SOCIAL MEDIA

**D**o NOT ignore this section – new statutory guidance for schools from 1 September 2022 means that schools actively search you out and may judge you by what they see.

So ask yourself the following question. Are your Social Media accounts presenting the professional image that you would wish a headteacher to see? Facebook, Instagram, Snapchat, Twitter, YouTube, TikTok, etc.

You may be surprised and even indignant that a prospective employer should stoop to spying on you in this way. However, not only is it perfectly legal, but now, from September 2022, the new Government publication *Keeping children safe in education 2022 Statutory guidance for schools and colleges* is actually advising schools to do so.

The statutory guidance says: "*As part of the shortlisting process, schools and colleges should consider carrying out an online search (including social media) as part of their due diligence on the shortlisted candidates. This may help identify any incidents or issues that have happened, and are publicly available online, which the school or college might want to explore with the applicant at interview.*"

So what will schools be looking for? Examples of offensive or inappropriate jokes, language and behaviour, especially discriminatory comments, inappropriate photos, evidence of illegal activity including drugs, even alcohol abuse. And above all, anything that suggests that the candidate may not be suitable to work with children or young people.

Also, this again is important, they will want to look for anything that might impact on the reputation of the school, academy, or Trust. Do we want our students or parents to see this about a teacher? Will our institution be brought into disrepute if we were to appoint this applicant?

A school or college will need to ensure that they do not use the information they find to discriminate unlawfully against a candidate. It is legal to do the search, as long as the decision about short-listing or employing you is not linked to discovering a protected characteristic under the Equality Act: age, disability, gender reassignment, marriage and civil partnership, pregnancy and maternity, race, religion or belief, gender, and sexual orientation.

So deciding not to call you for interview because you are pregnant, Muslim, Jewish, black, gay, etc., is illegal. But disliking your photos of raves, your derogatory comments on colleagues, your laughter at your SEND pupils, your unpleasant jokes, your X-rated photos, is a different matter.

No, not you, I'm sure! But I know of two members of SLT - not just teachers, senior leaders - whose unwise postings on social networks led to one being bullied out of his job and the other being viewed disapprovingly by the Chair of Governors who felt that having every photo posted involving a bottle, and having parents as friends, showed a lack of judgement.

And of course there is the not insignificant matter of the Teachers' Standards, where it says:

*Teachers uphold public trust in the profession and maintain high standards of ethics and behaviour, within and outside school.*

You therefore need a thorough review of everything associated with you online. Overall you need to be doing three things. Firstly, tightening up your privacy settings, secondly checking and deleting all negative impressions, and finally ensuring that you have some positive interests shown.

On Facebook, for example, get rid of anything in the *About* section that may not be in your best interest – groups you have forgotten about, books that you have liked in your teens – and consider how many photos you need of parties that you barely remember. You can also ensure that you have one or two education-linked interests.

Be equally strict in removing photos, tweets, videos, comments anywhere else that you would not wish to be seen by the headteacher. Or by your grandmother, I always think that something that you would not show to your grandmother should not be publicly available.

Look back at that quote from the statutory guidance: *This may help identify any incidents or issues that have happened, and are publicly available online, which the school or college might want to explore with the applicant at interview.*

You could be asked in interview about items that they found about you on line. That should encourage you to take my advice seriously.

# E-MAIL ETIQUETTE

E-mail etiquette is the next area in which to show professional standards. You will have abandoned some time ago the cool e-mail address that you had in your youth; what you need for applications is something that has your surname and either your first name or your initial in it. The best ones will have been taken by now, probably, so you should get something similar with a number added, such as John.Brown97@gmail.com or Jane.Green001@yahoo.co.uk. Make sure that the display name - the one that comes up when someone receives an e-mail from you – is correctly spelled and has capital letters for your name and surname.

When writing to a school, always put the job for which you are applying in the Subject line. When they look down the list of incoming e-mails they will therefore see:

**Jane Green    Teacher of French with Spanish**

Very clear and easy for them.

For communicating with a school, the body of the e-mail should be treated as a letter and set out formally and courteously. I once, as a headteacher, received an application where the e-mail to me, the headteacher involved in the process of appointment, began: *Hi Theo!* Oh dear!

Begin formally with the name of the person who is receiving the applications, and state again which post you are applying for. Don't put anything else in the e-mail except the post, the list of attachments (such as application form, supporting statement, summary, monitoring form), and a polite signing off.

Some people feel obliged to repeat part of their application in the e-mail (or worse, add extra information). Don't. It will either not get printed out and be lost effort, or it *will* get printed out and look messy.

# YOUR REFEREES

I dentifying your referees is the next thing to do. You will, as a NQT, have your University tutor plus somebody from one of your Teaching Practice schools. Other candidates will have their current headteacher (if you are the current headteacher, see later on in the SLT applications section), and somebody else who can speak in support of their application. This could be another member of SLT, a head of department, a key stage co-ordinator, etc. It could even be someone from a former school, as long as that was no more than 2 or 3 years ago.

Some people believe that you cannot have two referees from the same school, but you can; much better than out-of-date references.

In a large school you may believe that the headteacher doesn't know you; don't worry, they will ask someone else who does know you to help draft the letter. Again, if the headteacher has only recently joined the school and hardly knows you, you still put them as your referee. Another middle or senior leader will be asked to draft the reference, which will then be signed by the headteacher. For church schools, a reference from a parish priest is sometimes requested too. See below under faith schools.

There are two very important points about the choice of referees. First, you must give your current headteacher. If you don't, it will look very fishy, and the school may well contact them anyway, even though they were not given as referees. That is if they don't just reject your application for this reason. I once received an application where the current headteacher was not given as a referee, and the current employment was given as *"primary school in West Yorkshire"*. An obvious attempt to prevent me contacting the headteacher. Binned.

# HOW TO TELL YOUR HEADTEACHER THAT YOU ARE LOOKING ELSEWHERE

The second point is that you must speak to your referees and ask permission. You must not just put down your headteacher without telling them that you are applying for other posts, and hope that they will write a nice reference. If the first that they hear about your job search is when they receive a reference request, then they could be in a less than positive frame of mind for writing in support of your application. The same goes for your key stage leader or head of department; even if they are not your referees, professional courtesy requires you to tell them personally.

You may feel a little reticent about going to see the headteacher about this, and unsure what to say. My suggestion is that you tell them that you really appreciate working in their school and having such excellent colleagues, and have benefited enormously from all the opportunities for professional development, both formal and informal, that you have had.

However, the time has now come to move on to make the most of your development/an exceptional opportunity has cropped up to solve your problem of long commute and distance from your partner or ailing Mother, so you will, regrettably, be applying for a post at another school and hope that they will agree to be the first referee. They cannot really say 'no'. So be brave and go to see your headteacher.

Another important tip if you are doing supply teaching is to try to avoid using a supply agency as a referee, as their references can be pretty minimalist. Extremely minimalist. *We can confirm that Theo Griff has been placed in schools by this agency as a temporary teacher of Sanskrit since September 2021.* That's it – the whole reference! So do try to use two school-based referees if you possibly can.

# 4. DEFINING YOUR PERSONAL PROFESSIONAL CHARACTERISTICS

You now need to articulate your professional characteristics. In any job application, you are going to write about yourself, although it must always be in the context of what you will be able to do for the school. So you need to know what are your strengths, and what are your . . . well, let's call them areas for development! It's important to know these because your strengths must fit in with what a school is looking for. So sit down and work out what are your *Professional Characteristics, your Unique Selling Points, your USPs.*

# 360 DEGREE FEEDBACK

A good way to do this is to start by asking colleagues what they see as your strengths and areas for development – a 360-degree appraisal. 360 degrees because you ask those above you, your colleagues on the same level, and those whom you lead, if you are in a leadership or management role.

Once you have gathered these views, sit down and think: what it is that is special about you, things that make you a good teacher and a good colleague? The professional characteristics that you choose should reflect you, the sort of teacher that you are, what's important to you. Individual to you and to you alone, not applicable to 99% of teachers. It's important for you to ponder this and really decide what you are like, who you are, so that you can express this in your letter and later in an interview.

We shall look at these USPs later on in greater detail later on when preparing to write the letter of application or supporting statement.

# THE LEVEL OF POST THAT YOU SHOULD AIM FOR

**W**hich level of post is correct for you at this stage in your professional life, and therefore which jobs are and are not appropriate, needs to be considered. There is no point applying for something that is not suitable for you.

If you are just finishing your Initial Teacher Education or Training (ITET), then you will be looking for a post to do your induction. A post which is advertised as *NQTs welcome, Suitable for NQTs* or *NQT induction offered* is obviously for you, but you can also apply for any post that is on the MPR (Main Pay Range), including those with Inner London, Outer London and London Fringe payments.

If a post has a TLR (Teaching and Learning Responsibility) payment attached, it is not for you, as this normally requires someone to lead and support other teachers, with line management responsibility for a significant number of people. An advertisement that says *TLR available* could perhaps be appropriate as this means that they might decide to appoint someone without this responsibility.

Are you thinking of **moving into middle or senior leadership**? Many teachers looking to move forwards in their careers are unsure whether they have yet acquired the skills-set and experience to apply for a TLR post such as second in department, head of department, key stage co-ordinator, or pastoral leader.

There may be similar uncertainties when considering moving into senior leadership. To carry out any of these roles you need both the ability, and the credibility, to lead and support your colleagues, but not necessarily always the direct experience of every single task on the job description.

To test if you have the required credibility for the post, try talking to a colleague who already does the job and see what their view of you is. Also ask yourself if you have similar experience to theirs *when they started.*

As for your ability to carry out the required tasks, it would be unreasonable always to expect any applicant to have actually done already the job that they are applying for, so the shortlisting and appointing panels will be looking for experience in similar tasks, or other signs that you have the potential to carry out their role effectively.

Therefore, your first step in deciding if you should apply for a particular type of post is to do some research in general about what schools are looking for in their candidates. Go to an online teaching jobs website (e.g. TES, Guardian, eteach) and choose a post advertised anywhere in the UK which is the sort of job that you are considering. Read carefully the job description and think where you have shown the ability to complete these tasks, or could do them with appropriate training or guidance. Then look very carefully at the person specification to see if you comply with their requirements.

At first glance, you may think that you do not in fact meet their needs, but put on your thinking cap. If they need someone who can *demonstrate commitment to the values of the school*, remember all the extra support that you have done, and the ways you have made extra effort to help your pupils not just academically but also by always modelling correct behaviour.

Of course if the person specification says that an essential requirement is *Successful experience of developing new whole-school policies*, or *Ensuring progress in more than one key stage*, and you haven't done this, then becoming involved in initiatives such as these could be your next professional development target in your own school, so that you can acquire the experience and skills for the sort of post that you wish to aim for.

What if you are not applying to move forward, but moving sideways or even taking a step down?

Then you need to come clean, acknowledge that you are not on the normal career path at the moment, and say why. Briefly; don't make a big deal of it, but don't ignore it either. If you are giving up, say, a head of department or senior leadership role, explain, for example, that it is because you now realise that interaction with pupils is the most rewarding part of the job for you, and you regret the reduced contact time in your current role.

It is very important not to either write in the application nor say at interview that you just want a teaching job with no extra responsibilities. Instead of thinking from the point of view of what you want to get away from, what it is that you don't want to do, it is better to turn this on its head and look at what you DO want to do. This is what a school wants to hear, so this is what you want to concentrate on, what it is about their school that appeals because of how you would contribute.

A sideways move will similarly need an explanation, so be honest and say that their school is particularly attractive to you (but do NOT say that you hate your current one!) because it offers specific opportunities for you to support pupils and contribute to the school overall, or because you wish to re-locate for family reasons so are seeking to consolidate your current career position in their school in a different region, or just wishing to gain experience in a different school.

What I am saying here is that you shouldn't just fail to mention anything that might make a shortlisting panel query your application. Be open, don't hide anything, but don't go into a long, involved, explanation.

# THE MOST APPROPRIATE TYPE OF SCHOOL FOR YOU

**W**hich type of school would be right for you is the next question. There are a confusing number of different types of school; you could probably teach happily in more than one of these, so there's no need to be too picky. The schools divide into two wide categories: state schools (often called maintained schools) and independent schools.

State schools – those funded by public money – are the most numerous. The different types of state schools are basically defined by who controls them and how much freedom they have to set staff pay and conditions, or follow the national curriculum.

Community schools are controlled by the local council with no influence from a church or other religious group; they include infant, junior, primary, middle, secondary and special schools, as well as grammar schools. This is what we normally mean by a state or maintained school.

Foundation and voluntary schools have fewer constraints than community schools, as the local council has no direct control; these may include all the types of school as above. Faith schools are usually but not always foundation or voluntary schools, although more of them are becoming academies.

Free schools are state-funded but aren't run by the local council. They have more control over their own staffing and curriculum, as do academies.

Academies also are totally independent from the local council. Run by a governing body or trust, they may be part of a group. They do not have to follow the national curriculum, although their pupils sit national examinations. They have their own staffing structures, conditions and pay.

Independent schools are just that: independent of the local council and not state-funded; they get their income from charging fees, so are often also called fee-paying schools, private schools or public schools. A public school is in fact private; this term is used for the old-established independent schools, traditionally all-male boarding schools, although nowadays most have day pupils and some also admit girls too. The independent sector is very varied, and the conditions of work and pay for teachers can vary a great deal between different schools.

Ofsted.  The other issue that you may wish to consider under the heading of which type of school might be the current Ofsted rating of a school. Don't all rush to apply for Outstanding schools – you may find more support, more satisfaction (as well as perhaps more pressure) in a school graded 4.

If teachers are unsure whether a type of school is right for them, it is usually because it is a faith, free or independent school, or an academy, so let's look at these.

# 5. FAITH SCHOOLS

# GENERAL CHARACTERISTICS OF FAITH SCHOOLS

There are community, foundation, voluntary, free and independent schools, and also academies, which are classed as *faith schools.* The official definition is a school with a particular religious character or formal links with a religious organisation. About a third of all state-funded schools are faith schools, of which over two thirds are Church of England and less than one third are Catholic. There are 40 plus Jewish faith schools, a dozen Muslim ones and a handful Hindu.

# DO YOU NEED
# TO BELONG TO
# THE FAITH?

Faith schools are allowed to use religious criteria to give priority in admissions to children if they or their parents practice a particular religion. Of greater interest to teachers seeking employment is the fact that **faith schools are also permitted to select for employment on religious grounds**. They don't have to, but they *may*.

Voluntary-controlled religious schools can ask for a religious commitment in appointing, remunerating and promoting one fifth of teaching staff, including the headteacher. In voluntary-aided religious schools, the governing body employs the staff and can ask for this commitment in appointing, remunerating and promoting all teachers. In addition, teachers can be disciplined or dismissed for conduct which is 'incompatible with the precepts of the school's religion'.

The application forms for teaching posts at many Catholic schools include wording similar to this:

*Senior Leadership posts – Applicants are advised that the 'Memorandum on Appointment of Teachers To Catholic (Voluntary Aided and Independent) Schools', provides that 'the posts of headteacher, deputy headteacher and Head or Coordinator of Religious Education are to be filled by baptised and practising*

*Catholics'.*

*Teacher posts – Applicants are advised that schools/colleges are entitled to give priority to practising Catholic applicants.*

However, there just aren't enough practising Catholic teachers to staff all the Catholic schools. In particular, there are insufficient practising Catholic teachers who are suitable applicants for leadership posts, and the same applies to Church of England schools. This is easily seen by the fact that most years, up to 45% of all leadership posts in Church of England schools have to be re-advertised at least once, and over 60% in the case of Catholic schools.

From these statistics you can take heart on two fronts: firstly, that you do not need to be a practising or committed member of any particular religion to be appointed to a faith school (except for head, deputy head or head of RE), and secondly, that if you are, you have a better-than-average chance of ending up as headteacher!

# APPLYING TO A FAITH SCHOOL

S o how do you support your application to a faith school if you are not a committed member of that religion?

Since the overwhelming majority of faith schools are Christian of one sort or another, my comments will refer to them; they may be transferable to other types of faith school.

A key point will be referring in your application to the school ethos and how you can support and or contribute to the ethos/faith identity of the school. In both your application and any interview you will need to support what you say with concrete examples of how you will do this. Think about you and your pupils' contribution to form time or year assemblies in secondary schools; in primary, it will probably be whole-school assemblies.

Think also about preparing them for specific religious festivals during the year. Even if you are not in any way a practising Christian, you may still feel comfortable about leading form prayers and generally supporting the ethos of Christianity. Here is the sort of thing – but please do not copy this.

*Promoting positive values amongst my pupils is something that as a Christian I do constantly. Grungy Grove primary school, whilst not a church school, is a values-based school and we ensure that moral values underpin our daily life. I believe*

45

*that children should feel secure and happy in their school environment, and always be encouraged to make a positive contribution to society, both inside and outside school.*

Read what the two main faith websites say about the religious ethos of their schools; read both the Church of England and the Catholic one, as the general underlying principles are very similar.

If you are applying to a Catholic school, do research the Diocesan website for the area that the school is in and check out the most recent Section 48 inspection.

A number of faith schools ask for three referees, saying that the third should be your parish priest. So what if you don't have one? If you are a member of another religion, you can put your Rabbi or a respected member of the Gurdwara, etc. For other teachers, I suggest that you put there someone who can give a personal, not professional, reference. Not your Aunt Jemima, but someone who can state that you are of good character.

However, do not be dissuaded from applying to a faith school if you do not have a third referee. In a Catholic school application, it normally states that the third referee is just for practising Catholics; if you are not a practising Catholic then a third referee would not necessarily be expected.

# 6. FREE SCHOOLS

# GENERAL CHARACTERISTICS OF FREE SCHOOLS

F ree schools are state-funded schools, independent of the local authority. Any suitable sponsor can make an application to establish a free school, including parents, teachers, charities, academy sponsors, universities, community and faith groups, businesses and indeed other schools, including independent schools. The latter can also apply to convert to free school status to receive state funding, although it is said that 100+ have had such an application rejected.

In Summer 2022 there are over 600 free schools open and another 150 plus in the pipeline, many with the word "Academy" in their name. Do check the status of a school, therefore, as it may not be immediately obvious that it is a free school.

Free schools are free of many constraints. However, these constraints have been introduced into other schools over the years specifically to protect pupils, teachers and other staff. There is therefore some concern over the amount of freedom that the free schools have, as it could be abused. Check what your Union says about them on their website.

A free school:

Can be set up in any type of building, including disused

shops, hospitals and offices, as long as the premises comply with Health & Safety regulations

Operates independently of the local authority, as does an academy

Does not have to comply with the same rules as community schools in setting up its governing body

Sets its own pay and conditions for staff

Can employ teachers without QTS (unless they are coordinating special needs education, or are responsible for looked-after children)

Has to teach a 'broad and balanced' curriculum, but can develop and deliver its own curriculum, not following the national curriculum

Sets the length of its terms and its school days

Is subject to being inspected by Ofsted

Must offer membership of the Teachers' Pension scheme to teaching staff, and the Local Government Pension scheme to support staff

Ideally, the pay and conditions for teachers in free schools would mirror those in the maintained sector. But they often do not, so beware.

# 7. ACADEMIES

# GENERAL CHARACTERISTICS OF ACADEMIES

Academies have had bad press, as in the beginning they were failing schools. Now academies can be very successful schools, and deciding not to apply to a school that has become an academy could be limiting your choice quite severely, as there are so many of them now. In some areas, indeed, all schools are academies. And even if a specific school isn't an academy yet, it could well change. Therefore, the best advice is to treat an academy just like any other school that you might be considering applying for, and research it thoroughly to see if it is suitable for you.

# PAY AND CONDITIONS

One of the major areas for you to investigate in an academy is that of the pay and conditions of employment. Like free schools, academies could, in theory, pay you almost nothing and get you to work all the hours of the day. A big part of the teaching unions' objections to academies has always been that they do not guarantee that they will maintain the favourable pay and conditions that have been won for teachers over the years.

It would be useful, but pretty unlikely, to have the following information before accepting, or even applying for, a teaching post in a free school or academy.

What is the starting salary?

Is there pay progression?

Is progression related to performance?

How is performance assessed?

Are there any additional payments for additional responsibilities?

What are the normal working hours?

How many teaching hours per week are required?

What PPA time or equivalent, are teachers entitled to?

How many after-school meetings take place per year?

What are the term dates?

What are the holiday arrangements?

Are teachers free out of term?

What extra-curricular activities are expected of teachers?

What is the sickness policy and a teacher's sick pay entitlement?

What is the maternity/paternity/adoption policy?

And the pay entitlement for the above?

What notice are teachers obliged to give?

Is it the same for receiving notice?

Does the school have a clear redundancy policy, if it needs to lose staff?

What are the cover arrangements, do teachers do more than rarely cover?

Is there Union recognition in the school?

# UNION ADVICE
# ON ACADEMIES

T he NEU has a statement about academies. *The NEU is opposed to academisation yet supports and represents its members in academies in the same way as members in local authority-maintained schools.*

On the NEU website there is a very useful section on academies and their pay and conditions. I would urge you to read this so that you know what to expect if you are thinking of applying to an academy.

# 8. INDEPENDENT SCHOOLS

# GENERAL CHARACTERISTICS OF INDEPENDENT SCHOOLS

I ndependent schools can seem very attractive, as they often offer longer holidays and smaller classes, and more PPA each week, which must mean a lower workload, mustn't it? Yet this can often be offset by a longer school day and more evening commitments, including Parents' Evenings every term for each year group.

Yes, some independent schools pay more – much more – than in the maintained sector; but it is also true that there are some small independent schools which pay less, and do not even give the same sick pay, maternity pay, etc. as you would get when working in a community school. And there are now independent schools that are opting out of the Teachers' Pension Scheme. So beware!

As a former headteacher of a large HMC independent school, I know how the independent sector works, but your only source of information may be some tall tales and a few anecdotes. Is this the right sort of job for you? Would they even want to employ you?

Let me give you a clue about that last point: an independent school is generally looking for just one thing: an outstanding teacher who is deeply committed to the welfare and progress of pupils and their academic and personal development. Not so different from other schools, in fact. Having said that, it is true that a few schools will always be looking for degrees from Oxbridge, but generally outstanding teachers are what is wanted in the very best schools.

I am sometimes asked questions such as: "What are the pay and conditions for an independent school?" as though the schools were all the same. No they are not – they are independent, individual, individualist even, and something that is true for one is almost certainly not true for another. Below you will see some information about the different types of independent school that you might consider working in, but remember: they are all different.

# DIFFERENT TYPES OF INDEPENDENT SCHOOLS

**B**oarding schools. Would you enjoy working in a boarding school? The obvious difference is that the pupils aren't away by four, and someone has to supervise evenings and weekends, usually on a rota system. Supervision could mean just that: merely being there. But you might also be expected to be in charge of activities, getting them to put down their phones to play a game or some sport.

The schools generally pay extra for this – quite substantial amounts in the case of the big public schools – and often give free or highly subsidised accommodation, although there may well be tax implications here. The schools usually have shorter terms, which can counterbalance the extra hours you put in with your weekly duties. The pastoral career route in a boarding school can be very interesting, with deputy housemaster/mistress as a first formal step after being a member of a boarding house staff.

**The gender mix.** The single-sex schools, both all-boys and all-girls, include some of the top academic schools in the country. But there are also some all-girls schools which are small and a great deal less academic, concentrating as much on pupil welfare and supporting their personal development as on their academic curriculum. Single-sex teaching is different from mixed – whether or not you like it only you can tell.

**Belonging to a recognised organisation.** Pay and conditions – the latter including the amount of teaching you are expected to do, how late you stay there each day, whether you work weekends – will vary immensely between schools, but if the school is a member of one of the recognised organisations HMC, GSA, IAPS and SofH, you should expect overall pay and conditions to be at least as good as in the maintained sector. So membership of one of these organisations can be an indicator of reasonable pay and conditions. In other independent schools, this may not be so.

Some schools may not be in these organisations, being owned by an individual, a couple or a family, who have this as a business. Sometimes the owner is the headteacher. These can be warm and caring environments for both pupils and staff, but may on occasion be financially less sound, especially if they are very small, and may not always offer the same conditions of service as do other independent schools.

You may find, for example, that they do not always pay into the Teachers' Pension Scheme, nor give the same sick pay or maternity pay as teachers get in the maintained sector, and the pay may be less too. Check it out before you accept a job, or better still, before you even apply.

**Big and small schools.** Independent schools come in all sizes; a quick look at the Independent Schools Council website finds a school catering for years 7-13 with fewer than 100 pupils overall, and another which has years 9-13 with over 1,300; one has 20 times as many per year group as the other. It's a case of what you feel comfortable with, bearing in mind that any school will need sufficient pupils to pay salaries this year, next year, and into the future.

**Age groups.** Maintained schools (with the odd county that has dug its heels in for middle schools) are either infant, junior (or combined as primary), or secondary. Independent schools sometimes organise the age groups differently, and give them different names.

Pre-prep can be from aged 2 up to 5 or 6

Prep can be from 4-11, or 7-11, or 7-13

Senior can be from 11-16, 11-18 or 13-18 – the latter mainly big public schools for boys.

Many schools are all-through schools, ages 4-18, with a prep or junior school that feeds into its senior school. The term "secondary school" is not generally used in the independent sector.

**School groups.** Although I said at the start that independent schools are individual, there are some which are in groups. These may be small groups – perhaps just a boys' independent school and a girls' independent school with the same name and the same Governing Body - but some are quite large.

Being in a group can mean more financial stability and greater opportunities for professional development. For school leaders at middle and senior level it can be good to be in a group, as you have colleagues to discuss issues with; for heads in particular this is an advantage. A couple of the groups have been expanding into sponsoring academies, so have a maintained-sector arm too.

Among the best-known groups for independent schools are:

Cognita

GEMS

GDST – Girls' Day School Trust

United Learning

Woodard

# APPLYING TO AN INDEPENDENT SCHOOL

A s with free schools and academies, the best advice is to try to find out as much as possible about the pay and conditions before you apply. It can be tricky to do this; your best bet for all these schools is to e-mail the Business Manager or Bursar and ask.

To try for anonymity, you may think that it would be best to do so from a completely different e-mail address than the one that you will use for any application that you may subsequently make, one that does not include your name. But don't then include your name in the enquiry that you make in the body of the e-mail, as that would give the game away.

You may find that the independent school that you intend to apply to has a slightly different procedure for applying from that of a maintained school. They quite often require a CV, and may not have an application form. In that case, your application will consist of a CV, a letter of application, and an executive summary, all of which are explained further on in this book.

When applying to an independent school, you will need to remember that they are not just looking at your teaching experience and success, but will expect you to make a contribution to the wider school life and activities. It would be appropriate to include a paragraph in your statement or letter outlining how you feel you would contribute; start by looking at the website and seeing what is already on offer in the co-curriculum. Is there anything there where you feel you could support an existing activity or could offer a new one? You don't have to be a whizz at sport and have coaching certificates (but if you do, so much the better), as there are very many other skills that would be appreciated.

# 9. PREPARING TO APPLY

# WHEN TO APPLY FOR A JOB

B e aware of both the normal starting dates and the required resignation dates. If you are already on a permanent teaching contract, you will need to abide by the contractual resignation dates. For maintained schools in England and Wales these are 31st October, 28th/29th February and 31st May to start in a new school the following term. If you are not currently working in a school, these dates won't bother you.

Some people think that you just have to give half a term's notice to leave your school, that you could resign by 1st September and leave at the October half term. However, it is not normally possible to leave at the end of October or indeed at any other half term, in any type of school (community, academy, free, independent), as there is no provision in the School Teachers' Pay and Conditions document for this, nor in contracts for most schools that don't follow the STPCD.

Another warning: teachers often think that you have to resign by the end of the half-term holiday, but you should note that the exact last dates for resignation are the last days of the respective calendar months. Do take care here; you don't want to miss the deadline just because half term rolled over to the next month.

Independent schools generally follow the maintained

sector over leaving dates, i.e. you cannot leave at half term, but the majority of them require a full term's notice for their teachers, so you have to tender your resignation on or before the first day of term. You will need to read your contract carefully – is it on or before?

These resignation deadlines mean that the teaching jobs are, as much as possible, advertised in time to allow other teachers to resign and join a new school. So end of September for January, mid-January for Easter, and from March or April onwards for the September start.

There will also be advertisements at shorter notice, when a teacher resigns on or just before the deadline, say 28 February, for instance, and the school will be hoping to get a replacement for the summer term. This means that just after the resignation dates there will be more advertisements, but only those teachers not employed on permanent contracts will be able to apply, since everyone else has missed their resignation deadline.

This could be good news for you if you are unemployed, someone wishing to return to teaching, or on a short-term contract that is coming to an end, wishing to return to the UK after a period abroad, and also for any NQT still job hunting in June.

Independent schools, having longer notice periods, tend to advertise at least half a term earlier, with jobs for September starting to be advertised from October onwards, and quite heavily from January or February for the new school year in the following September.

For leadership posts, the dates are different again. In maintained schools, the contractual resignation dates for heads are a month earlier than for teachers; in the independent sector you may have to hand in your resignation two terms or more before your leaving date. Check your contract is always the answer. For SLT posts there are two peak periods for advertisements for September starts: mid-October to mid-November, and then the major peak of mid-January to early May. A deputy headteacher post may have to be advertised when a serving deputy headteacher has just been appointed to a headship, so they tend to be a little later in the advertisement season. There are further details on this in the SLT applications section.

In the independent sector, leadership posts are often advertised 4 terms ahead for headship, and three terms ahead for deputy posts.

Once you have got the right time of year, have now identified your USPs, the level of post and the types of school that would all be appropriate, you can start looking for vacancies to apply for. At this point, you may start considering the location: near where you already live, somewhere else where you would wish to move, or would you be happy finding a job just about anywhere in the country?

**Think through the location carefully**. Inner-city schools are very different beasts from rural ones, as is living in these areas. Consider above all the commute; how will you travel to school, how long will it take?

**Think about the size of the school too**, especially in primary. Small schools are very different to larger schools. In small primary schools, you may be asked to take on more responsibility and be expected to multi-task. While this provides excellent professional development through hands-on experience of a range of aspects of school life, it can also mean that life-work balance can be compromised, especially for middle and senior leaders.

# WHERE TO FIND THE TEACHING VACANCIES

Obviously, you cannot apply for a post unless you know that a vacancy exists; except for some special cases, writing speculative letters to schools is not likely to help you get a job nowadays; you need to be proactive in finding out about job vacancies, so that you can apply for them directly.

The TES online is where you get to the jobs faster, either by just logging on via your computer, or with the TES Jobs App – it's free to download for both iPhone and Android. With the App, once you have input your selection criteria (area, phase, subject, level of post) you get information updated every day about the jobs that are appropriate for you. You can also set this up via your computer.

There are jobs in other publications too. Local papers tend to be better for part-time or cover and other temporary posts, although some schools advertise permanent full-time posts there. The Catholic Teachers' Gazette also publishes vacancies that may not always appear elsewhere and these teaching vacancies (apart from head, deputy and head of RE) are open to candidates of all faiths. The Guardian Jobs has a large number of teaching vacancies, but be just a bit wary, as some weeks a lot of these seem to be placed by recruitment agencies, not directly by schools themselves. Which brings me to . . .

Agencies will often tell you that they can certainly get you a job in a school, sometimes even adding that they have a special arrangement with a school that guarantees you an interview. However, although this may be true for hard-to-appoint posts (A-level physics, for example) unless the school is recruiting for a post, such as a headship, where the only way to apply is through the nominated agency, it can be a bad idea to take this route for a job application. Why? Because schools have to pay the agency an introduction fee on appointment. You can see that if a school has a choice between candidates who cost nothing or a candidate who could cost them several thousand pounds, they are more likely to put the agency candidate to one side.

If you are limited in your geographical search, another place to look is the websites of the nearest local authority or authorities, as many of them post their teaching vacancies there. In some areas, a number of local authorities have clubbed together to advertise all their jobs; a good example of this is the West Midlands Jobs Portal. The first time you use this portal, it can be tricky to get to Education and then Schools/Academies, Teaching roles, and your subject or key stage, but once you've got the hang of it, it's good. It also gives you the vacancies by area.

A number of local authorities use *Pools*, especially for NQTs in primary. This is a centralised system for recruiting to induction posts, a bit like UCAS – you make just the one application for all the schools in that local authority. You need to look at each local authority in the area that interests you, and check very carefully the pool closing dates, as some are before Christmas for the following September.

The essential point that you need to understand about pools is this: you don't get to choose the school, the school chooses you. Of course, you can turn down the offer if you don't like the school, but may then risk going to the end of the queue for job allocation.

# HOW TO RESEARCH A SCHOOL BEFORE APPLYING

R esearching the school is the next step, once you have found a possible job to apply for. The aim of the research is twofold: first, to see if it is the right school for you, and second, to enable you to show in your application that you are the right person for them, that you are exactly the teacher that they are looking for.

A deputy headteacher says: *Make sure that you research the school. Schools say similar things about their aims and ethos, so it's more useful to read the newsletters and scrutinise the calendar.*

You should first read very carefully all the information that they send you. Use a highlighter pen (or equivalent on your computer if you are keeping the document there) to identify what seem to be the key aspects of the school overall, plus any specific things they may be hoping that the appointee could contribute.

Next, you should go through the school website. Generally, the same key aspects will come out there, confirming what you highlighted in their paperwork, perhaps expanding on the points. What you see on the website will help you to build up a picture of how the school sees itself and where it sees itself going. These key aspects of the school, and how it sees itself, where it sees itself going, will need to be addressed directly in your application to show that you understand the school ethos and will contribute to it.

Do also look at external sites where the school is featured. Clearly, the inspection report (Ofsted or Independent Schools Inspectorate) will give you more details about the school, but do be wary of quoting from the report in either an application or an interview. You can seem bumptious and big-headed if you are not careful. They know perfectly well what it said, may have already addressed any areas for concern, and certainly do not want you to suggest that you are the fairy godmother arriving to wave a wand to solve all their problems.

The BBC Education league tables website can provide useful insight into a secondary school, as does the Department for Education website, especially the School Performance tables which have a lot of data including comparisons with other local schools (very important for independents) as well as schools nationally. You can estimate from this where a school places itself in the pecking order.

If it's a local school, then dropping in to the high street estate agents and asking which are the popular local schools, and going to buy in the local newsagent's and asking what they think of the school and its pupils, can provide some interesting information.

A Google search for the school will show how it appears in the local press, but don't believe everything that you read.

A better way to find out about the school is, of course, to visit during school hours before application, although this isn't always possible.

# VISITING A SCHOOL BEFORE APPLYING

During the pandemic, school visits became a lot less common, a trend which has continued in some cases even now that there are no longer any restrictions. Read this section nonetheless to see what might crop up during your application for a post.

Pre-application visits to schools are fine if you can get there easily. A handful of primary schools make visiting a prerequisite for consideration for a post; basically, if you don't visit, you don't get shortlisted. This is unfair on those who live too far to visit, on those who cannot spare the time to go, (because of childcare or because they are teaching and cannot be released), or are doing supply and would lose a day's pay.

A common reason for being unable to visit is that your current school will not allow you to visit in school time. Some teachers believe that they have a right to visit a school where they are applying; the truth is that unless you are being made redundant, you normally have no right even to go to an interview against your Head's wishes, yet alone just go to visit a school before applying. Not even in your PPA time.

My advice is to talk to colleagues and see who could cover for you in exchange for you doing them a favour, and when you have therefore a possible solution to your absence, go and see your headteacher with the request and solution together.

So should you visit before applying? You do need to try to go by what the school wants, within reason. Many schools encourage visits but do not insist on them, which is both sensible and fair. There are three points to bear in mind about school visits:

1. Should you make the effort to visit before applying?

2. What if it is impossible for you to visit?

3. What should you do, and what question should you ask, during a visit?

Whether or not you try to visit before applying depends on the school; if they mention visits in their advertisement or details, then you should go if possible. Phrases such as: *Visits welcome, Please contact to arrange a visit,* or *We encourage you to visit* mean that you should try your best to go and see the school.

On the other hand, if there is no mention of visits for a classroom post, then don't. It tends to be maintained primary schools who expect a visit; independent schools, with a few rare exceptions, do not expect or wish for visits, and many independent schools would be taken aback if you did ask to come to see the school. They will normally arrange a full school tour, often accompanied by two or three older pupils, on the day of the interview, so you are not going into the interview with no feel for the school.

So unless the details say something about visits, generally you shouldn't ask for one.

Senior leadership positions are different; many schools, both primary and secondary, say that they would welcome visits, or give a phone number to contact someone to discuss the post. This means that you really do need to ring or visit to get as much information as you possibly can to use in your application.

However, there are many very good reasons why people

cannot visit. I would hope that a school would understand this, and make allowances.

When a school has encouraged visiting but you cannot get there, it's a good idea to say in your application that circumstances precluded a visit, but that you have researched it well, and feel that you know the ethos, and similar brief comments. It's also a good idea to contact the school by e-mail, explaining that you cannot visit and asking if someone might be available to speak to you by phone. Once arranged, you must ensure that you have a few questions ready, based on your research.

In the application letter, you then ask for Mr/ Mrs/ Whoever to be thanked once again for the time they took to speak to you by phone as you were unable to visit as you would have liked. This explains your failure to visit, and shows your interest.

What sort of things might you ask in this brief phone call? For example, if they are looking for skills or a contribution in a particular area that you can offer (someone to play the piano for Assembly? a lunchtime Spanish club?) followed by a brief query about one or two things you have noticed from the application pack, their website, etc. Do all your research before the call and have a pen and paper to hand to note down the answers that you get. Always make it to the point and be brief – you don't wish to seem as though you are trying to show off or impress.

Because showing off and trying to impress is a very bad idea in any contact with the school. It is one way that going to visit a school can turn out to be to your disadvantage.

I often get asked what candidates should do and ask during a school visit, and my reply is always *nothing*. By that I mean, of course, nothing to make yourself stand out and nothing to try to impress. As a rule, we find this off-putting.

Dress smartly, be polite, pay attention, smile at people.

Interact positively with any pupils that you meet, perhaps make a brief comment on something good that you see, if you can do so casually. However, you shouldn't feel that you have to draw attention to yourself. As for asking a question, unless it is essential to know and could make you decide not to apply (e.g. I am Jewish and in the winter months I need to be home before nightfall on Fridays, for Shabbat. Would it be possible for the timetable to allow this?), then don't ask anything.

Nothing is worse than a candidate pulling out a list of questions that are either of minimal importance (*which desk will I have in the staffroom?*) or designed to show off (*can you tell us how you have addressed the areas for improvement highlighted in the recent Ofsted report?*).

If you are individually asked if you have any questions, ask one that has occurred to you if it's important; otherwise don't scrape the bottom of the barrel trying desperately to find something to ask. It's fine to say: *No thank you, I have all the information that I need for my application.*

Only if that's true of course, and it should be if you have done your homework. If you haven't done your homework, you could look a fool asking something that is in their documentation, or on their website.

Or worse still, a stock question often suggested by your university tutor: *Can you tell us what you did in your training days last year?*

Why on earth do you want to know that – so that you can sit down later and revise what you missed? At this point I will say again that few, if any, University tutors have experience in appointing staff to schools, so their advice should be listened to politely but not considered to be wisdom from the horse's mouth.

Final point: a pre-application visit is really an interview. I, and many other heads, have rejected applicants before they apply because of inappropriate behaviour, dress or comments in these visits. The candidate who is unfailingly courteous (starting with the way that they speak to Reception staff), pleasant, friendly and professional yet quietly contemplative rather than rushing at every opportunity to get a word in before anyone else does, is more likely to impress us.

Once you have decided that this is a suitable school for you to work in, and have identified their key features, you are now ready to start writing your application.

# 10. THE APPLICATION: GENERAL OVERVIEW

T he aim of an application is very simple: it is not just to get shortlisted; it is to get shortlisted as the favoured candidate. This means that when you walk into the interview room, the panel is already so impressed by you that you are the person that everyone else has to beat. Your application must convince the school that your experience, qualifications and capabilities offer the best match with its job specification, and should showcase your unique qualities and experiences that will benefit the school. Your USPs.

# THE 4 MAIN ERRORS TO AVOID IN AN APPLICATION

T here are, generally speaking, four main errors made by candidates in their applications. I go into these points in greater detail elsewhere, but let's just look at them briefly now:

1. Not applying for the right job

2. Not following instructions

3. Not understanding what it's all about

4. Not making it easy for the school

Not applying for the right job we have looked at above, but beware also the danger of applying for multiple jobs at the same school, giving the impression that you are a Jack-Of-All-Trades, but master of none. I have received applications from people asking to be considered both for a post in my junior school and for teaching A-level. How can I take that seriously?

Not following instructions? Well, what can I say about that? One simple thing is often due to following the advice of your University tutor, who on occasion tells you to write *See letter* on the application form instead of filling it all in. No, please don't do that. If we ask you to fill in the form, then just do it! Other fairly common failures include the letter or supporting statement being too long or too short, or not your own work, or leaving gaps in your chronology.

Not understanding what it's all about – it's about what you can do for that particular school, how they will benefit by appointing you, not the other way round. That should be the overarching theme of your application. Remember that famous quote by John F. Kennedy?

*Ask not what your country can do for you; ask what you can do for your country.*

Avoid, therefore, enthusing about how this school will provide you with the ideal opportunity to consolidate your skills and move on from your current post. I am quite sure that you would not have thought of telling me, as did one applicant, that you wanted to work here because it is conveniently situated for your daughter's primary school. It's what you can offer the school that counts.

Finally, some candidates just do not make it easy for the school to even consider their application seriously, yet alone appoint them. So make everything legible, give full contact details for everyone, have a clearly structured letter of application or supporting statement, and of course, include an executive summary.

Before we look at the different elements of an application, let's look at whether you are an internal candidate.

# THE INTERNAL CANDIDATE

W hen a vacant post is announced in your school, it may be restricted to internal candidates only, or it may be advertised externally, with other candidates also applying.

In both cases, you need to show yourself to be an outstanding candidate who meets all the school's requirements.

If the post is purely internal, this can sometimes be a little harder to do than if you are competing with external candidates, since there may be little or no information available about the post and what they are hoping for in a successful applicant. For an external post, on the other hand, they probably prepare both a job description and a person specification.

So the first task, if it's internals only, may be trying to discover what is involved in the job, what skills and experience it is useful to have, so that, firstly, you can assess if you are an appropriate applicant, and secondly so that you can show this in your application.

That first item is quite important. On too many occasions, people desperate for promotion will apply for any and every post going in their school, whether or not these posts are suitable for them. This can be counterproductive, because when that person finally applies for what is the right post for them, they have often ruled themselves out by their poor judgment previously.

So start by approaching both your line manager and the person currently holding the post that you are aiming for (they may be the same person), and ask what qualities are needed to carry out this role successfully. Ask also what experience they themselves had when they first began in this position. After all, it would be unreasonable to expect applicants to have every single experience and skill right from the start.

An internal vacancy may well have a less formal applications procedure. No application form, and you are often just asked to write a letter to the headteacher outlining your suitability for the post, or even to write an *Expression of interest.*

Avoid the trap of thinking that for an internals-only application, you can just sit down and dash something off. Make it formal, begin the letter to the headteacher *Dear Ms Greening*, and work on the letter or expression of interest so that it shows how you fulfil all the requirements for the post.

Avoid the second trap of misunderstanding the wording *Expression of interest*, which is in fact a supporting statement. It should indicate clearly your skills and experience, how you meet the criteria, not merely stating that you are interested in the post.

And how long should the letter or statement be? Unless it says otherwise, two sides A4 in a normal-sized font with normal-sized margins. Do not be tempted to crowd more into a cramped layout with narrow margins or a tiny font. Personally, if it's hard to read, I am tempted not to read it.

Whether it is an internals-only application, or one where you are in competition with external candidates, there is one very important final trap to avoid. Very often, the major failing of internal applicants is that of under-selling themselves. They can tend to think *"I don't need to tell them that – they know what I do".*

Oh yes you do need to tell them that! You need to set out everything (within reason – not minor or irrelevant points) just as you would when applying for a post in another school where they don't know you and your achievements at all. This is not only absolutely essential when applying for an externally-advertised post in competition with teachers from outside, it is also important when applying for an internals-only post. Your motto should always be: apply as if to another school where I am unknown.

This, by the way, also applies to the interview – tell them everything, don't rely on them remembering what you do. And even if they do remember it, if they are using a fair score sheet to assess the interview candidates, what you don't tell them will gain you no credit in the scoring. Remember that.

It is very common for internal candidates to fail just because they didn't sell themselves.

# SPECULATIVE LETTERS

A speculative letter, one where you write to a school that has not advertised a post, saying that you would like to teach there, and setting out all your details, used to be popular. Popular with teachers, anyway; I am not so sure about schools, although I myself was once offered a job on the spot nearly 50 years ago when I walked into a school and asked if they were short of a teacher. A speculative letter in person, and it worked.

However, speculative letters and unsolicited letters of application nowadays very rarely do achieve their aim, and one of the roles of the school secretary is normally to weed those letters out of the morning post before the pile is handed to the headteacher. This means that the headteacher generally doesn't even get to see them, as they are considered an inappropriate way of appointing staff.

How likely is it that a school will say: *We need a teacher. I know! Instead of advertising and getting a good range of applicants, let's just ask that chap who wrote to us a few months ago to come along, in case he hasn't got the sense to look out for our advertisement!*

There are two reasons why schools generally do not use speculative applications. Firstly, they are anxious to get a good selection of applications, so that they can select the most promising for the interview. Therefore, instead of going to a filing cabinet full of unsolicited applications, they advertise.

Secondly, they wish to be fair to everyone, and to be seen to be fair. Just consider this: you were hoping for a vacancy to teach Spanish to come up in your local school, heard that there was a teacher leaving, but no job was advertised. You then learnt that the job had been given to someone else without advertising. What would your reaction be? Therefore, schools publicise their vacancies through advertisements as part of a fair appointment procedure.

It is also part of the general issue of safeguarding to advertise rather than just give a post to someone.

Is it nonetheless worth sending a speculative letter? Although there will always be someone who assures you that this is how they got their job, my view is that in general it is not. The only time that it could be useful would be if they had a sudden urgent need for a teacher (their member of staff taken seriously ill, for example) and your letter just happened to turn up, or if you can teach a subject in high demand – A-level physics or mathematics for example – and they are expecting a vacancy and want to tie you in with a contract before you go somewhere else.

# 11. AN EFFECTIVE APPLICATION

# THE 3 MAIN PARTS OF AN EFFECTIVE APPLICATION

T here are three main parts to an effective application, in addition to any other things that the school may ask you to send in, such as an Equality Monitoring form. These three elements are:

1. An application form

2. A supporting statement or letter of application

3. An executive summary to show how you comply with the criteria, that you are what they are looking for.

# THE CURRICULUM VITÆ

**Y**ou may be thinking *What about the Curriculum Vitæ – don't I need a CV?* For some years now the statutory guidance to schools has been to ask for a completed application form rather than a CV, to ensure that all candidates provide the same information in the same format. However, independent schools, academies, free schools, teaching agencies and international schools may occasionally ask for a CV.

In these circumstances, if you did the preparation that I outlined earlier, your qualifications and professional appointments files will be a good starting point. If you are asked to send a CV, send a version that is complementary to other components of your application, and is no more than 2 sides of A4, unless it is for a SLT post when more will usually be appropriate.

A Curriculum Vitæ should include:

1. Personal details: name, address, full contact details, NI and TRN. Your age and gender are not needed, except occasionally for international schools, nor is your family situation

2. Education and qualifications: teaching qualification, degree subject and university, A-levels & possibly GCSEs

3. Employment record: names of schools, dates, post held.

Most recent first.  Give your responsibilities /achievements

4. Referees with full contact details by as many means as possible

# THE PERSONAL
# MISSION STATEMENT

In your Curriculum Vitæ there should be no personal mission statement. Nor anywhere else in your application. *A highly qualified and enthusiastic teacher looking to work in a fast-paced environment where I can give of my all.*

No thanks.

# 12. THE APPLICATION FORM

U ntil the blessed day when local authorities, academy chains and individual schools get together and finally agree on a UCAS-type standard form for every teaching post, you are going to have to fill in a lot of application forms, all in different formats. Many of them seem designed to make you crazy. Here are some tips to keep your sanity.

First of all, when you receive a form by e-mail, save it to your computer with a new filename that includes your name, as I explained earlier in the section about organisation.

Remember, if you just keep it with their filename, then when you send it back to the school they won't know whose it is without having to open it and read your details. And even worse, they may just save it to their computer where it will overwrite their master blank form, and then they could send out your completed form with your carefully crafted supporting statement to the next hopeful candidate who requests a form. It has happened, as I told you earlier.

Do they expect you to fill in the form online? If not, if it's in Word but is password-protected and you cannot write in it, then e-mail the school to ask if they could send you an open version. If it's in PDF, you could try downloading some software to help you, or try an online converter programme. I like http://www.pdfonline.com/pdf-to-word-converter. Or again you could ask the school if they have a Word version.

# HOW TO FILL IN THE APPLICATION FORM

I t is important to remember two things about filling in the form. Firstly, fill in everything, do not leave blanks (Contribution to wider school activities – nothing at all?), nor, worse still, write *See letter*. Advice from University tutors sometimes suggests putting this; please don't! A school wants all the information from its candidates in the same format and in the same place. If you can't be bothered to get the information from your letter and fill it in here too, then why should I bother to go and look for it? Make it easy for me to see that you are a good candidate, not hard.

Similarly, don't be coy and decline to fill in your current salary if they ask for it. Failure to do so just annoys, and you don't want to annoy the school before you even get to interview.

The second thing is that everything that you put on the form, or indeed in any other part of the application documentation, must be truthful and honest. The provision of false information in an application is an offence which could have serious consequences, including prison.

So do not exaggerate your qualifications nor your contribution to an initiative in a school; do not try to hide a job where you walked out of the school after just 1 month by fudging the dates of other posts, do not try to pretend that the job in Barcelona where they asked you to leave at half term was actually just part of time spent travelling abroad.

I am sometimes asked how to fudge a difficult issue in an application; my advice will always be to come clean and explain the situation honestly but briefly. Further on there is a section about applying for a teaching job from a potential position of weakness.

Application forms are notoriously fiddly to fill in, and they seem to ask for different information, or want to have it presented differently. There are some constants, however. If you have done your preparation before starting the application process, you'll have all your details of dates, schools, N.I and TRN numbers, CPD, together with full contact details for your referees, all together in one place, to make it easier to fill in the form.

I mentioned earlier one thing that you may no longer have, if you have been in teaching some time: details of the starting and leaving salary of all past jobs. Yes, some schools ask for this! You'll just write *Information unavailable* in that case; this is not going to impact on the success of your application, so don't worry.

**Do check carefully** what they wish you to fill in, and how to do it. Do they want your education or job history in chronological order, or with the most recent first? Is there a separate box for your Current Employment, or does it go with your Employment History?

NQTs in general will not have a professional Employment History, of course, just your education. When applying for an induction post, you may include under Employment your Teaching Practice in a school while doing your PGCE at a University, but making it very clear that it was TP, not employment.

For subsequent applications, you shouldn't put in your TP, the exception being if you are applying for a post in a very different type of school from your current one, and did a TP there. So if, after three years teaching in a comprehensive you are now applying for a post in a Grammar school, you could include your TP in a Grammar school, while making it clear that it was not actual employment.

You may also have some voluntary work that is relevant to education, or part-time work while you were studying which is not at all relevant. However, when filling in a form, applicants are required to include details of all employment since leaving school, for Child Protection reasons.

If from age 16 to the end of your PGCE you were waitressing and working on a checkout at weekends and in the summer, it's going to fill the form with too much irrelevant information. Any permanent job that you may have had, for those of you doing teaching as a second career, needs to be included briefly on your application form. I have seen an application where the candidate gave four pages of detailed information about his time in the Forces, and summed up twenty years in education in two lines. Poor judgment, irrelevant, and boring.

But for all those part-time jobs, just sum them up like this:

*June 2016 – Aug 2018: Part-time temporary posts in retail and catering whilst in full-time education*

Any gap in employment also needs to be included and explained in your Employment History, including non-employment when bringing up children.

Some of the questions that you are asked may puzzle you, especially if they are initials. NOR for a school is Number on Roll – how many pupils it has. *Are you a member of GTC?* is still quite common, as is asking for your GTC number. This just means that they are using an old form, not having revised it since the GTC was abolished in March 2012. Just put N/A.

Similar out-of-date requests may include asking for your DSFC or DfEE or DFE number. As we said earlier, here they mean the TRN (Teacher Registration Number) which is found on your QTS certificate, so that's the first place to look for it.

# ASKING FOR REFEREES NOT TO BE CONTACTED YET

O n the form there's the important request for the names and contact details of your referees; you should have this all to hand in your neatly organised files. At this point you may wonder if you can ask them not to request references unless you get an interview. The short answer to this is: you can sometimes, but it is not advisable, especially as some schools will turn down your request, and in fact discard your application.

Application forms for teaching used to follow applications for other jobs, and have a box to tick if you wanted to be informed before they contacted one or both referees. That has now generally been removed, as the statutory guidance to schools is that they should always obtain references before interview, so that they can discuss with you any doubts or issues. Here is the extract from *Keeping children safe in education (2022), Statutory guidance for schools and colleges*

> *221. The purpose of seeking references is to allow employers to obtain factual information to support appointment decisions. Schools and colleges should obtain references before interview, where possible, this allows any concerns raised to be explored further with the referee and taken up with the*

*candidate at interview.*

*222. Schools and colleges should:*

*• not accept open references e.g. to whom it may concern*

*• not rely on applicants to obtain their reference*

*• ensure any references are from the candidate's current employer and have been completed by a senior person with appropriate authority (if the referee is school or college based, the reference should be confirmed by the headteacher/ principal as accurate in respect of any disciplinary investigations)*

*• obtain verification of the individual's most recent relevant period of employment where the applicant is not currently employed*

*• secure a reference from the relevant employer from the last time the applicant worked with children (if not currently working with children), if the applicant has never worked with children, then ensure a reference from their current employer*

*• always verify any information with the person who provided the reference*

*• ensure electronic references originate from a legitimate source*

*• contact referees to clarify content where information is vague or insufficient information is provided*

*• compare the information on the application form with that in the reference and take up any discrepancies with the candidate*

*• establish the reason for the candidate leaving their current or most recent post, and,*

*• ensure any concerns are resolved satisfactorily before appointment is confirmed.*

References are a very important part of the appointment

procedure, as you can see from the above.

You are happy with a reference being requested if they are definitely going to interview you, but perhaps would prefer them not to ask without warning you, to give you a chance to tell your referees that you have been applying for jobs. You therefore like the idea of that box to tick.

You may find that a school is still using up old forms, and that box is still there, but I don't suggest that you tick it. From the point of view of a school, having to get your agreement before asking for references is a nuisance. For starters, it makes more work for them, yet another thing to do. They have organised a streamlined plan for all the tasks involved with the appointment, and you upset it all.

Then it slows down the process. They have to contact you, then wait until you have spoken to the headteacher, then contact your referees (and at a different time from all the other referees they are contacting interfering with a planned working day with a different task) and wait for the reply.

This is a minor annoyance for the school, but the major reason for not requesting them not to contact your referees just yet is that it could suggest that you don't have a very good relationship with your headteacher as you haven't told them that you are applying. See what I said above.

This request may not seem like a big deal and perhaps individually these reasons are not, but a school very hard-pressed, in a hurry, or very sensitive to good staff/SLT relationships, could have second thoughts about you if you are equally weighted with another candidate for shortlisting. In the worse outcome you could lose out all together, at best be seen as a bit awkward before you have even got into the interview room.

Heads report that they sometimes receive forms with incorrect email addresses and incorrect telephone numbers, which makes it extremely difficult, frustrating and time-consuming when requesting references for several candidates. Their solution? *I do not receive a favourable impression of such a candidate and am more likely to reject this application at this late stage*, says one headteacher.

# THE REASON
# FOR LEAVING

**A**pplication forms have a section for you to fill in all your teaching posts; this often has a final column headed *Reason for leaving.* Not very useful, in my view, but if it's there, you have to put something in it. The space is usually very limited, and the obvious thing to put is *Career progression* or *To progress my career.* That is why it's useless, of course, as that is the obvious thing to put. If you are, or have been, on a fixed-term contract then it is very easy just to write *End of fixed-term contract.*

My advice is that what you put here should always be honest, and my suggestion is that *Career progression* covers most innocuous reasons for leaving in an honest fashion. It is very important not to lie. If you put something on an application form that is later found to be false you may be summarily dismissed, so take care.

If you have a settlement agreement or agreed reference, read the relevant section towards the end of the book.

In general, there are certain reasons that it is best not to include on your form, or in any part of the application process, including the interview.

Some reasons are clearly inadvisable; anything that is negative towards your current school – or a past school - should not be anywhere. Resist the temptation to write *Personality clash,* or *Unhelpful colleagues,* or even *SLT did not control pupil behaviour.*

There are other reasons that it is preferable not to give, as they can be misinterpreted by the headteacher reading your form. The first of these is anything including the words *new challenge.*

When I read *To seek a new challenge* as the reason for an applicant wishing to leave their current post, I have an immediate reaction which is not in your favour, I'm afraid. It can suggest to me that you are jumping before being pushed. Or even that you are indeed being pushed.

Another reason that it is best not to put is *Personal reasons,* which can be interpreted as *I am difficult and don't get on with my colleagues.* If it is a personal reason, it can usually be honestly described as *Family reasons.* This covers just about everything, including moving to a different town to be with your girlfriend or caring for children or elderly relatives.

The expression *To widen my experience of different year groups* is not going to impress me either as the reason for leaving a permanent post if you are currently doing supply. Nobody gives up a secure income for the vagaries of supply merely to gain wider experience. If it's just moving between schools, this is fine as a reason, however.

But in that rather difficult situation of having left a permanent post for nothing, I wonder if it would be truthful and honest to say something along these lines: *Having realised early last term that the changing ethos of my school no longer matched my own, I decided at half term to resign for December, believing that I could get another post for January. However, no suitable post was advertised, so I am currently (working on supply/ doing volunteer work in X/ still job hunting).* Obviously, this will not fit into the little box on the form, so there you will have to put something bland and meaningless such as *Change of school* or *To seek new post*, or that good old standby *Moving on,* and then have the very brief explanation as part of your letter or statement. Make sure that you **do** include this explanation!

Including a very brief explanation of an unusual career trajectory (such as resigning and leaving a job for unemployment) is important because it could make the shortlisting committee suspicious. You don't want them to speculate and start imagining all sorts of weird and wonderful things.

So include something truthful but fairly innocuous in your application to put their minds at rest before they even start speculating: *14 years in St Paul's School, and she gives up that salary and that type of school for a fixed-term one-year post at Grungy Green Free School! Was she caught with her fingers in the ski-trip till?*

In circumstances where you are applying to a school in a new area, it can be useful to include a very short, one or two-sentence only, paragraph in your letter giving a brief reason. It could be that you are hoping to relocate for family reasons, or to be nearer your ailing Mother, your long-term partner, your old Granny, and have seen from the website of X school that you could make a specific contribution to their ethos/successfully lead on the new A-level syllabus/develop the girls' football team or whatever. You justify your intended move by looking at the post to which you are applying and give that as a reason.

1. Keep it truthful
2. Keep it brief
3. Keep it simple.

During your interview too, you may be asked why you left a particular post, or why you are seeking a new job now. More about this in the companion book I have written: ***Interview for a Teaching Job.***

# 13. THE LETTER OR STATEMENT

This is your chance to stand out of the crowd and show us who you are and why we should appoint you. Make it professional, but make it yours.

A deputy headteacher in Wales gives this advice to applicants: *Tell me all about your sporting interests, community involvement, talents that may be useful in a school beyond the classroom, such as playing an instrument or charity work. I want to know how you, above others, will contribute to my school and what gifts you can bring that I can harness and develop.*

The view of a secondary headteacher in the North West is: *I'm looking for an application that is well written - definitely no spelling, punctuation or grammatical errors and absolutely no 'text' language or colloquialisms - and is in the applicant's own words, reflecting their experience, philosophy of education and their reasons for wanting to work in my school. I do not want a re-hashed version of someone else's words or a generic statement that they're clearly using for other applications.*

# SHARING APPLICATIONS

A ny application letter or statement is very hard to write. You are tempted to get some outside help here. A friend or colleague has been invited to several interviews, but you haven't. It must be her letter of application; it must be the supporting statement that he included, and the great executive summary!

Wouldn't it be useful to borrow it to have a look? Not to copy of course, just to get an idea of what sort of thing to say, just to have an example to see the structure, the sort of thing to include. Yes, what a good idea!

No, it would not be a good idea. On the contrary.

First, it might cause your application to be rejected on first reading. You see, some local authorities are using plagiarism software, similar to that used by UCAS in order to detect non-original personal statements. If a sentence in an application is the same as or very similar to that in someone else's in the national database, then it is considered possible plagiarism and the advice from local authorities to schools is to reject such applications as one cannot tell who wrote it first.

As a result, if there is the slightest hint of plagiarism in an application, it could well go straight to the reject pile. You might not mean to copy it, but just reading an example of someone else's application can tend to leave a memory in your mind as you write your own. It is therefore best to avoid even glancing at another application.

Secondly, of course, the letter or statement or executive summary that you submit needs to be your own work so that it reflects accurately who and what you are, otherwise you might get a job in a school that doesn't fit with you as a person. To put it bluntly, it has to be about you and by you, because it will be you who will have to do the job in the end, not the friend who passed on their work.

The third reason for not looking at someone else's application is that they probably wrote it for a different school, so how can it reflect the criteria and values of the school that you are applying to? An application is about one specific person applying for one specific post in one specific school. There is no One-Size-Fits-All.

Another danger that doubtless will now have occurred to you having read the first point above, is the danger of allowing others to see your application. This is another example of something that is definitely not a good idea.

If I e-mail to my friend Susan my lovely application, and then I apply for another job using it, my application that I wrote so carefully could be rejected because of the similarities to an application put in by a friend of Susan's, to whom she kindly passed on my application, just as an example, not to copy of course.

Once you have shown your application to somebody, you have no control over where it will end up, and it could come back and bite you. If you look at an example application, you will most likely be influenced by it. Do not look at someone else's, and do not show yours.

So you know by now that I am not going to give you here a nicely prepared letter for applying for a teaching post. As a headteacher, I have indeed received two applications for a post with a near-identical paragraph in each, and rejected them both. I wish to save you from this fate.

# GENERAL ADVICE ON THE LETTER OR STATEMENT

No example here for you to copy. However, I am going to give you some general advice for writing that all-important letter of application or supporting statement.

An application must always include a supporting statement or a letter of application, whether or not you are asked for one.

*Keeping children safe in education (2022), Statutory guidance for schools and colleges* describes it thus: *a statement of the personal qualities and experience that the applicant believes are relevant to their suitability for the post advertised and how they meet the person specification*

So, letter or statement? There is no difference between the two, except that the former is in letter format. By this, I mean that it starts *Dear Ms Brown* and ends *Yours sincerely.* The statement just starts with whatever you are saying in support of your application.

This letter or statement is your chance to sell yourself as a professional who will make a positive contribution to the success of the school and its pupils. So it must be (a) professional and (b) relate to that school and its requirements. Don't have just one letter that goes to every school.

How long should it be? No more than two sides A4 in a normal-sized font is about right. But do check that the school hasn't stated what it wants; I saw one recently which asked for no more than one and a half sides.

# SUPPORTING STATEMENT, COVER LETTER, LETTER OF APPLICATION – AVOID THE CONFUSION

I f you are asked to send a statement, then you do not send a letter of application as well. A supporting statement is the same as a letter of application, so you can't have both. But if you send a statement, then you will need a cover letter, which is, in theory, completely different from a letter of application.

Be warned: some schools ask for a cover letter when they mean a letter of application. A cover letter acts as an envelope, is brief, and in no way supports your application. It will run something like this:

*Dear Ms Browning*

*Post of English teacher in Portsmouth Lane School*

*I wish to apply for the above post, and attach my completed application form, ethnicity monitoring form, supporting statement and summary.*

*Yours sincerely,*

*Anne Applicant*

Nobody asks for a real cover letter like that just quoted, so if they do ask for a *cover/covering letter*, then they really mean a letter of application, and that's what you need to provide. Don't send a cover letter as well as a letter of application, by the way. Just one letter.

So the possibilities are:

Application form that includes a statement + cover letter

Application form + separate statement + cover letter

Application form without statement + letter of application

And very occasionally:  CV + letter of application

# THE AIMS OF A LETTER OR STATEMENT

The letter or statement has several aims that you must ensure that yours can achieve.

1. To convince a school that your experience, qualifications and skills offer the best match with its job description and person specification

2. To illustrate your unique qualities and experiences

3. To get you shortlisted for an interview, and as the favoured candidate

4. Not to get you sacked subsequently, for dishonesty or because you can't do the job. It must therefore be honest and truthful.

# THE PROFESSIONAL APPROACH

T he letter or statement, to be successful, must be **professional in its appearance**, so that it impresses at first glance.

1. Sent as an attachment, not in the body of the e-mail

2. Appropriate font size and type: not Comic Sans, and not too small to read easily

3. Name and page number on every sheet in case someone drops a whole pile of applications

4. Appropriate e-mail address and filename, as explained earlier

5. No mistakes, nothing crossed out. The spelling, punctuation and grammar should be impeccable. Do not rely on a computer spell check for this, get some real eyes to proof-read for you, and be 100% sure that this person has excellent knowledge of spelling, punctuation and grammar

6. Professional appearance overall: white space with margins and line between each paragraph

7. Right length: 2 sides A4 normal-sized font, normal margins - but check if the school sets a limit

8. Addressed to the right person, right name, right

spelling, right Dr/Mr/Mrs/Ms, and at the right school. You would be surprised how many applications we receive that talk about another school.

The way to avoid missing the name of another school, if you are re-using part of another statement or letter, is to do three searches on *"School"*, *"Academy"* and then *"College"*. That will pick up every mention of a school in what you have written, and allow you to check that the name is the right one for this application.

**It must be professional in its content**, so that it builds on the positive first impression from the professional appearance.

1. It must be written for your audience in a UK school, so British and educational in style, not American or as though you are applying for a job in a large company. Beware of US internet guides, trite expressions and mission statements: *A forward-thinking professional aiming to work in an equal-opportunities environment where I can hone my skills . . .*

2. Take care that it is truthful, not exaggerated; try to back it up with evidence with measurable achievements wherever possible. *GCSE A--C increased by x%*

3. Do base it on your research: Ofsted or ISI, Local Authority, local demography, competitor schools, website – and above all the documents that the school sends you

4. It is best to have it structured like a good student essay, with headings. They are busy people, it will help them to grasp your major points, and will help you not to ramble; see below for this

5. Overall the emphasis will be not so much looking back at what you have done, but looking forward to what you will do for their pupils and the school overall.

This latter point is very important. I dislike the expression *personal statement* as it encourages an applicant to write too much about him or herself, instead of concentrating on what are the school's requirements and how they can be met for the benefit of the pupils by this specific applicant. Yes, you will talk about what you do, or have done, but *always in the context of what this school is looking for.*

# THE BASIC RULE

T he basic rule is that it's all about the pupils. What the school wants for the pupils, what you can provide for the pupils. I have seen applications with not one mention of pupils or students.

You should always write your letter coming from this angle of the benefit to the pupils, not about what's best for you. It's not about why you need them, it's about why they need you.

You think that's obvious? Of course, you won't be writing: *This job is very convenient because I can drop off little Johnny at nursery on my way in.* But you might be inclined to write:

*This job would provide me with the support that I need for my NQT induction year*

*This post would offer me a perfect environment in which to extend and develop my teaching skills and experience*

*Being appointed to your school would enable me to develop my professional skills to further my career in education management*

The school is not all that interested at this stage in what's good for you, it's more interested in what's good for its pupils, and if you can provide it. The letter or statement is your chance to show this.

N.B. you should check their documents and website to see

whether to say *pupils* or *students.* And then do a search on your document to check that you are consistent in your use of this.

# IDENTIFYING THE SCHOOL'S BUYING BUTTONS

What is a buying button? It is used in sales to identify what it is that the customer is looking for, so that when you press that button by mentioning this feature of the product, they want to buy. Different people – and different schools – may have different buying buttons.

A salesperson wishing to sell double-glazing to one person would push the BB of *You will save on heating costs.* For another potential customer, the BB might be *Won't the neighbours be impressed by your smart new windows!*

Find out what it is that the school wants for its pupils by reading all its paperwork and scrutinising its website and, if it has one, prospectus. What is it that the school is looking for? What are its values? What is really important to them? What can you do to help achieve this? If you can meet its needs, then ensure that in your application you say so clearly, pushing those buttons so that they want to buy the product – you.

An obvious buying button for most schools is *learning and progress for all*, but schools will word this differently (check their website) and have other aspects that are important to them. You'll include them in sections 3 and especially 5 below.

# IDENTIFYING YOUR UNIQUE SELLING POINTS

**K**now what you have to offer, and set that out in your letter. Remember, it's all about the pupils and what you specifically can offer them.

This is where you need to define fully your USPs. Time spent on this is important, as they will be useful not only in writing your letter, but also in preparing for your interview.

You now sit down to identify three (or possibly four) USPs. They have to be about *you*, not USPs that someone else has suggested, because they have to want *you*, because it's *you* who is going to have to do the job, fit in with the rest of the school, etc, so giving them answers that don't show *you* but someone else is just not sensible.

So think of your USPs; here are some examples of draft USPs, just to give you a general idea. They are not all perfectly worded yet – you don't have to get them right first time round, you do a first draft then polish them a bit so they are just right.

*I have good communication skills with parents*

*I am very committed to the pastoral side of working with pupils*

*I am prepared to work very hard for the children*

*I am very analytical and clear-headed*

*I am very caring about the whole child*

*I think academic success for all students must be our aim*

*I enjoy working cooperatively for materials preparation*

This is too many, of course, and anyway you should not copy any of these because it is very unlikely that they will be exactly who and what *you* are.

Do not despair at this point. I will say that it is very hard to think of your USPs; it almost seems like boasting, on the one hand, and also you are probably not used to doing this kind of self-analysis, on the other. But do persevere as it is very important to have these clearly in your mind. They will be very useful for your interview preparation later on, too.

Here are my USPs, me, Theo Griff:

*Committed and hard-working*

*High levels of analytical intelligence, you can't pull the wool over my eyes*

*Passionate about children, their welfare, their education, and their success.*

This is me now, not as a school leader but as an education consultant. If I were still a school leader, I would have different USPs to give. If I were still a teacher my USPs would be different again, because I would be at a different stage in my career, and also because out of a slightly larger number of USPs, all of them honest and truthful about me, I would select the most appropriate ones for this specific application.

Yes, you may need to select the USPs that you use, because another important point about your USPs is that they should match the school's BBs – their buying buttons, what it is that they are looking for, what they need for this specific post. Frankly if there isn't a pretty good match between your USPs and their BBs, it might not be the job for you, and you might not be the candidate for them.

Let's suppose that one of your USPs is:

*I have experience in three inner-city schools with a high percentage of pupils from varied ethnic backgrounds.*

That might well be a good match for the BBs of a school in Luton, but not for a school in rural Powys.

So be careful to identify what are the school's BBs and check the USPs that you choose to include in your application, and subsequently discuss in the interview, to ensure that there is a good overlap. And, of course, although you should read carefully their documentation and website, remember that there are hidden BBs, or at least BBs that are taken for granted. Standard BBs might be *Raising achievement, The whole child, The Catholic ethos,* etc.

Another thing that might not be in their requirements, but which it could be useful to offer, is subject flexibility. If the post is for a teacher of history, and you can also offer English to KS4, mention this. Maths and science flexibility is particularly welcomed in many schools, so look at your experience and qualifications and see how you can add an extra string to your bow.

Whereas in the interview the succinct version of your USPs can be used (there is a follow-up book: **Interview for a Teaching Job**), in your letter of application or supporting statement you will be expanding on them as appropriate, perhaps 2 or 3 sentences. They could fit in sections 3, 4 or 5 below.

# THE STRUCTURE OF THE STATEMENT OR LETTER

Having a clear structure enables you to respond to all their stated requirements coherently and shows that you have good communication skills. A rambling letter shows that you are neither coherent nor organised.

It's important to avoid giving the story of your education or teaching life. That's on the application form, and should not be in here at all. Nothing makes my heart drop more than reading an application that begins: *After doing my first degree in applied mathematics at the University of Leeds, where I got a 2i, I did my PGCE in Huddersfield and then took my first job teaching mathematics to A2 level in Greenhill College. From there I progressed to . . .*

How does all that – which I have already seen on the application form - show me that you are the teacher that I need? By including this, you are doing yourself two disfavours: putting in something inappropriate and wasting valuable space that could have worked for you.

**Headings are useful**. In particular, they keep you focused on what you are writing so that it can be logical and well-organised. If you feel uncomfortable about sending out a letter with headings, then put them in while you are drafting, to ensure that you keep on target in each paragraph, then delete them before sending them off. I'd leave them in, personally, as they act as signposts to the reader that you know what to write.

When I do individual consultations with teachers and look at their letters or statements, I often ask them to pencil in a heading for each paragraph. If they say that they can't, because there are several topics in one paragraph which cannot be summed up in a single heading, or if they have the same /similar heading for two paragraphs at different ends of the letter, this is a sign that the letter is not well structured and logical.

You might like to try that yourself with your most recent letter of application or supporting statement, and then award yourself a mark out of 10.

Which headings should you use? Use the person specification or job description main headings, if they are sensible. Sometimes they are not (I have seen almost as many poor person specifications and job descriptions as I have poor applications), in which case use something like this:

*1. (A first paragraph with no heading)*

*2. **Knowledge, skills and current professional experience**. Here you say what you are doing currently, but in structured fashion: curriculum role, pastoral role, managerial role, co-curricular, contact with parents, working with other schools, experience of budgeting, your pupils' achievements, etc. It is very important that you don't just talk about what you do, or have done, but show the* outcomes, *what you actually achieved, and how this could translate into the new school.*

*3. **Other achievements relevant to your post**. Include here details of your responsibilities or contributions in previous posts; any outside activities that show skills relevant to teaching and managing children and colleagues; any specific and highly relevant training done.*

4. ***Personal qualities and attributes***. *It should be quite clear what to include here.*

5. ***My contribution to your school***. *What you think the post is about, based on the clues that they give you. What do they need you to do? How would you fulfil this? This is your chance to show them that they need you.*

6. *(Final paragraph, no heading)*

This is just a suggestion for a possible structure; a completely different format might well suit you better. You might, if applying for a first teaching rather than a leadership role, wish to have sections about your philosophy of education, how you put this into effect in your teaching practice or current post, how you have been supporting every pupil to success, with examples, and what you would hope to contribute to the new school. That could make a good statement or letter.

You might even base your letter or statement on the major headings of the Teachers' Standards.

It is important to ensure that you mirror in your application the language that the school uses, addressing the points in their documentation, so that they can see clearly that you tick their boxes. The best way to ensure this is to do your executive summary before writing your letter, so that you are quite clear in your mind about what they want and how you meet this. See below for more information on the E.S.

When writing each paragraph of the letter or statement, always bear in mind that you are showing that you can provide what the school needs. You could, perhaps, sum up a paragraph by having as the last sentence something like *This is in keeping with your school's aim of having the highest academic expectations of its students* – obviously relating this to one of the points you have noted from its website and documents. Don't overdo this, though; in every paragraph it will look daft.

NQTs often find it very hard to write this letter or statement, because they have little professional experience. However, it should be possible. Here are some suggestions:

*Tell me about the teacher that you are, and will be in a year's time. Tell me what you've learned from your training so far and how you're putting it into practice in the classroom. Tell me what makes you better than all the other applicants. But tell me in your own words, not those you've trawled for on the internet,* says a primary headteacher in Sheffield.

## Salutation

You only have a salutation (*Dear Dr Griffiths*) if it's a letter, never in a statement.

Use the headteacher's name and spell it correctly; do not start *Dear Sir,* nor *Dear Madam,* and certainly not *Dear Sir/Madam*, nor *Dear headteacher.* Get the Dr/Mr/Mrs/Ms correct too. Ring up the school and ask if you are unsure, having first checked to see if it is on the website, on the headed paper, or elsewhere in the documents available.

N.B. even if you are an internal candidate, be formal here and address the headteacher by his or her surname. And address the letter to Ms Browning even if you visited the school and the headteacher encouraged you to call her Caroline.

## The first paragraph

Preface your letter or statement with a paragraph consisting of three or four sentences. Ensure that you start on a strong note by writing clearly, succinctly, and making an impact by addressing their needs. Your letter or statement should make the reader want to learn more about you, right from the beginning. Refer to the job advertisement, say briefly how you match this, and say specifically how you would contribute to the school, how you would be an asset.

Here is the sort of thing that I mean. I do not need to warn you not to copy this as others might also use it.

> *In making this application for the post of deputy headteacher of High Hills School, I offer you a breadth of skills and experience gained from my roles as a senior and middle leader in three schools of varying size and type. If appointed, I would expect to use these skills working co-operatively with other members of the senior leadership team to further enhance the student experience, to meet and indeed exceed parental expectations, and to consolidate the reputation of High Hills School as the school of first choice in the West Midlands.*

Here is another example:

> *I wish to be considered for this position and enclose my completed application form, summary and monitoring form. I am attracted to this post as a development of my role as second of the English department in which I have direct responsibility for the development and delivery of the KS4 curriculum, with specific emphasis on raising the achievement of boys. I now feel ready to extend this experience of supporting colleagues in improving pupils' learning into another school. School XXX is of particular interest to me because of its emphasis on ensuring that all pupils meet or exceed their potential through ………*

**The last paragraph**

Leave your reader with a final impression that is very positive. Conclude your statement or letter with 2 or 3 pithy sentences that remind them that you're a good match to their requirements. You might wish to reword your USPs, ensuring that they link with their requirements, showing that the school would be better if it appointed you.

> *I believe that I have the necessary experience, initiative and vision to fill the role of deputy headteacher at your school. The attached summary shows that I already carry out effectively the majority of tasks associated with this role. If appointed, I would use my skills to further strengthen the ethos of*

*the school and improve achievement, to develop the Learning and Teaching to respond to curriculum changes, and to provide the learning environment for every student to achieve their potential and thus further promote the outstanding reputation of High Hills School.*

And do be careful to write *Yours sincerely* at the end, not *Yours **S**incerely*. No capital.

Unless you have been able to insert it in the application form, put your one-page executive summary as page 3 of your letter, so that it is printed off automatically. More about this summary below.

Proof read the letter carefully, don't just rely on the spell check; it's a good idea to pass the letter to someone else to read, as a new set of eyes could spot something that you have missed.

# 14. THE EXECUTIVE SUMMARY

An executive summary is something that I started using – and advising others to use – some twenty or more years ago. Its name stems from the one-page briefing that a P.A. would give the boss for him to read quickly on the way to a meeting, setting out in an easily-digested form the salient points of an issue.

# WHAT IT IS

In the context of a job application, the executive summary (aka E.S.) is an at-a-glance way of showing a potential employer that you match their person specification, and that therefore you are a very appropriate candidate who should be shortlisted.

# WHY YOU SHOULD INCLUDE ONE

I t is highly unlikely that you will be asked to include an E.S. in your application, although I have seen one or two cases. So why should you go to the trouble (and I will warn you that it is difficult) of producing one when they don't ask for it? Because it makes it very clear to the shortlisting panel that you are exactly what they are looking for. As simple as that.

I have been told by Governors, headteachers and H.R. professionals how much they appreciate and value a good summary with clear evidence. When I was hosting the TES advice forum for jobseekers, there were posts from both candidates and headteachers about the quality – or otherwise – of applications.

Time and time again teachers said that in their interviews they had been particularly complimented on the E.S. Here is one such comment received:

*The deputy headteacher said 'thanks so much for doing this (executive summary) you'd be surprised how many people don't and it makes our job so much easier'*

And another:

*The Chair of Governors singled out my executive summary as an excellent addition that made shortlisting me easy.*

Headteachers also posted saying that they wished applicants would do a summary, and also that they would follow my advice in general:

> *Have spent the afternoon short listing and one of the candidates had clearly studied Theo's advice. A good letter, a clear, precise executive summary. Matching this candidate to the person specification was a doddle.*
> *I heartily recommend you read Theo's advice and you should sail through the first round.*

Another said:

> *Short-listing today. One (yes only ONE!) Executive Summary! CPD hidden in letter of application TWICE with "See letter" on application form! Two small font, close typed A4 pages within the "Other relevant experience" box! Why oh why do people do this? The whole panel was complaining. Do yourselves a favour and FOLLOW THEO'S ADVICE! She knows what she is talking about! Rant over!*

An HR professional in a large Academy chain said:

> *A well written summary is an invaluable part of the selection process. It sets out clearly the applicant's skills and experience, and matches it exactly to what we are looking for, enabling the selection committee to shortlist fairly and impartially by our stated criteria.*

You can now see why you should do an executive summary: it's because it sets out very clearly exactly how you meet their criteria, and therefore helps them to see that you should be shortlisted. It also ensures that when you write your letter of application or supporting statement, you are very clear about what are the school's priorities and how you can address them.

So always do your E.S. before you start drafting that letter or statement. It is also useful for you as an aide-mémoire when you go to the interview. This is why they should shortlist you and this is also why they should appoint you.

# WHEN NOT TO SEND AN EXECUTIVE SUMMARY

There is one occasion when you should not send an executive summary as part of your application; this is when the school specifies that you should not include additional paperwork. In this case, do the summary anyway, to help you write your letter or statement, and as an aide-mémoire for the interview, but don't forward it to the school.

So what exactly is the executive summary, how do you do one, where do you include it in your application?

# HOW TO DRAFT THE EXECUTIVE SUMMARY

An executive summary is a two-column table. In the left-hand column are their criteria for appointment, and in the right-hand one, your evidence in brief note form that you meet their requirements. Its aim is to do their task of shortlisting for them, because that generally is how we shortlist candidates.

The normal procedure for shortlisting is that we draw up a large table with the criteria in the left-hand column, then a number of columns, one for each applicant, where we go down putting a tick or cross next to each criterion, finally putting a Y or a N at the very bottom of each column for whether we wish to invite them in for an interview.

# EXAMPLE OF TABLE USED BY SCHOOLS TO SHORTLIST CANDIDATES

| Criteria | Candidate 1 | Candidate 2 | Candidate 3 |
|---|---|---|---|
| Qualified to teach and work in the UK | ✓ | ✓ | ✓ |
| Good Honours degree in main subject | ✓ | X | ✓ |
| Successful teaching to GCSE and A-level | ✓ | ✓ | GCSE only |
| Evidence of driving up standards of achievement for all | ✓ | ? | ✓ |
| Effective behaviour management | ? | ? | ✓ |
| Commitment to regular ongoing professional development | ✓ | X | ✓ |
| Shortlist Y/N | Y | N | ? |

There are several very important points about an executive summary. It must be extremely well presented, so that it communicates immediately to the reader your suitability. It must have appropriate and strong evidence as your proof of meeting a criterion, otherwise it is only emphasising your ineptitude. And, (with the possible exception of a SLT application) it must be one side of a page only. It also needs to have your name on it, and the word *Summary*. Not executive summary, just *Summary*.

How, therefore, do you draw up an executive summary for a job application? You start by examining the school's person specification, noting which criteria are essentials and which only desirables; unless you have something extra-special under the desirable heading, you can usually omit all those points. You wish to keep it to just one side, remember? It may also be appropriate to use some of the job description, including tasks that you already carry out well.

You will omit a criterion for which you have no evidence; if it asks for "*At least three years' experience teaching GCSE*" and you have only two, don't include that in the summary where your failure to meet that requirement will attract their attention.

However, if there are several areas where you fail to meet their essential requirements, then you should consider seriously whether you should be applying for this post, as it could be said that you are not a suitable or credible candidate. That is why it's a good idea to draw up a quick draft executive summary, just jotting down first ideas, if you are uncertain if a post is right for you. Or if you are right for the post.

With a bit of luck, after weeding out a few minor criteria, you are left with a dozen points for which to find evidence. See below for what to do when you have a very long person specification.

The great thing is that the left-hand column is exactly what they are looking for because it comes from their person specification or job description. How can they fail to shortlist you if you tick all their boxes with highly relevant examples showing excellent experience?

The main – and most difficult - stage is finding these highly relevant examples of what you do or have done, to include as your evidence.  This can take quite a long time for the first-ever summary, but it gets easier with time. A first-time-ever executive summary could easily take two or three hours to do.

Do not give in at this stage - it's all worth it! Remember that quite a lot of the evidence that you have gathered for this executive summary will be used in subsequent applications, so the effort is not wasted. It is also preparation for the interview, so overall the time is very well spent.

When you feel depressed or even disheartened over this difficult task, just re-read above the comments by the headteachers who appreciated getting an executive summary in an application. It could make all the difference to your application.

Now write "Your requirements" as a header on the left column, and "My skills and experience" on the right, and enclose the summary with your beautifully crafted letter of application.

Below is a possible example of part of an executive summary.  I will give my usual warning here: you should most certainly not copy anything that is on there; many other job seekers will read this, and you don't want to have your summary reminding a headteacher of theirs, leaving you open to accusations of plagiarism.

# EXAMPLE OF PART OF AN EXECUTIVE SUMMARY

| SUMMARY | |
|---|---|
| **Theo Griff: Post of Class Teacher, KS2** | |
| **Your Requirements** | **My Experience** |
| • Qualified Teacher | • QTS and PGCE Primary (with Merit), University of Exeter, June 2011 |
| • Experience in teaching KS 2 | • Have taught Year 6 at Two Mile Hill Primary for 3 years |
| • Competence in teaching in KS1 | • Successfully completed NQT induction year in KS1; occasional teaching in Year 2 |
| • Familiarity with working with EAL children | • Work alongside a specialist EAL teacher at Two Mile Hill Primary where over 90% of my class speak EAL <br> • Currently developing support materials for a Syrian refugee pupil |
| • Ability to work as part of a team | • Work as a team with TA, CT, volunteer TA, parallel class |
| • Ability to use ICT and IWBs | • Confident user of IWB. Integrate ICT in to lessons as appropriate, including pupils' use of IWB, laptops and scanners |
| • Evidence of relevant CPD | • Attend Child Protection, Safeguarding and Prevent training every September. Other CPD topics covered include Raising achievement in Maths, Creative writing, KS2 Science and SATs |
| • Communicate effectively to a range of audiences | • Led Inset on new SATs for 17 colleagues from 3 schools <br> • Communicate well with parents and carers on a formal and informal basis |
| • Trustworthy with a commitment to respecting confidentiality | • Maintain confidentiality when working in conjunction with Police and Social Services <br> • Aware of safeguarding and school policies in the event of disclosure being made |

# PROBLEMS IN DRAFTING THE SUMMARY

So far, so good. You take the essentials from the person specification, find your evidence, put the summary together. But what if the person specification has a very large number of essentials? Or even worse, there is no person specification at all?

If the personal specification is very long, then you need to do the following:

1. **Prioritise.** What are the most important things for them? You should be able to see that from their website or other documentation – their Buying Buttons for a start. And if you are short of space, leave out things that can be seen easily from the application form, e.g. QTS

2. **Condense.** On the example above, there was a whole sentence for each of their requirements; these have been cut down to the essential words, so that they fit in a narrow column and leave more room for your evidence

3. **Combine.** Often there are similar requirements that you can put together. "The ability to communicate confidently on paper or e-mail with all members of the school community" and "Confidence and self-assurance as

a speaker in different situations" could easily go together. Combine and condense them to make "Assured speaker and confident communicator, both orally and in writing".

A school sometimes does not have a person specification for a post; this would be unusual for a middle or senior leadership post, but it is not unknown for classroom teacher positions. It may have a job description which can serve, although that may not be much use either, so you are in a slightly difficult situation here when a school doesn't actually seem to be very clear itself about what its criteria are. One wonders how it can select candidates in that case.

Not having a person specification shouldn't stop you from doing an executive summary, however.  You obviously cannot have the first column headed "Your requirements", as you don't know what their requirements are.  If it is a middle leader post, such as a Key Stage co-ordinator or head of year, you can do a search, for example on the TES website in the Jobs section, and find a similar post which does have a person specification.

I am tempted to say that you should then apply for that job instead, since that school seems actually to know what it is doing, but I realise that it might not always be a convenient commute for you.

An alternative – and always my choice for a classroom position - would be to use the Teachers' Standards.  This gives criteria such as "Set high expectations which inspire, motivate and challenge pupils"," Promote good progress and outcomes by pupils", and "Demonstrate good subject and curriculum knowledge".

Change your left-hand header from "Your requirements" to "An effective KS2 teacher" (or whatever the job is), and then do the executive summary based on the Teachers' Standards, or the alternative similar job that you found as suggested above.

It might actually be worth doing a Teachers' Standards executive summary anyway, as preparation for any interview where you might be asked how you meet these standards.

# WHERE TO PUT
# THE SUMMARY

If there's a space on the form, put it in there; quite often there's an expandable space called *Additional information*, and this would be very appropriate in that position. If there isn't a suitable space, then put it at the end of your letter, as the third page, so that it gets printed out automatically.

A final point: you should note that the E.S. is not instead of your letter or statement, it's as well as, it's an addition. Form + letter + E.S.

# 15. APPLYING FOR A SENIOR LEADERSHIP POST

A ll the advice given above about applying for a post in a school is also applicable to SLT applications. What comes next is an addition to that. If you have come straight to here, go back and read the earlier part too.

## Background reading as preparation

Your bedtime reading, for all level of SLT applications, should be the *Headteachers' Standards (2020).* This is where the serious thinking begins. How many of these key characteristics can you honestly lay claim to? Possibly more than you think, actually; really think hard about possible examples of your practice which could support a SLT application; you'll need those later when you come to do your executive summary and interview preparation. Download the very handy *Headteachers' Standards 2020: self-assessment tool*

Of course, if you realise at this point that too many of these characteristics still need further development, then instead of a blueprint for an application, the Headteachers' Standards document now becomes a route map for your own professional and personal development over the next year or so.

But supposing that you can tick, at least faintly, most of

the characteristics, then in many ways this is a good time to be applying for senior leadership posts: year on year, the number of re-advertisements of leadership posts seems to be increasing. This is good news for you as it means that there are insufficient suitable candidates, or that candidates are not presenting themselves as suitable. Either there is less competition, or you can take specific steps to beat the competition by effective presentation. Read on.

Before you go any further, you might find it useful to know what the procedures are likely to be. In 2012 the National College for School Leadership as it was then produced a useful guide called *A guide to recruiting and selecting a new headteacher*. In December 2016, The National College for Teaching and Leadership (National College) produced – or re-published - a similar guide to recruiting and selecting a new headteacher. The National Governors' Association also has interesting documentation available. Familiarise yourself with all this, even if you are applying for an assistant or deputy headship, as this will set the general context for your application too.

Another document that it would be useful to read can be found by Googling *A-governors-perspective-applying__-for-senior-roles-in-education-2014*. When you actually find it, it's called *Applying for HT/DHT/AHT roles*, but a search under that title will not find it. This has some interesting insights.

As with any application, you begin with the preparation, including planning your campaign to obtain the leadership post, starting with the timing. A crucial point for preparing your application.

# CALENDAR OF VACANCIES

For several years, I counted every week the senior leadership vacancies that were advertised in the education press. Maintained, academy, free and independent schools in the UK, all age ranges, for assistant headteacher, deputy headteacher and headteacher posts. You may substitute *principal* for *headteacher* in all of those job titles. I am setting out below the result in a chart for September to July.

From this you can see that you should start to plan your preparation for a senior leadership application several months before the peak period, allowing sufficient time to ensure that when the advertisements start, you have all your basic preparation completed. Remember to check your own resignation dates, especially if you are already in the leadership team, or are working in an independent school, as they may well not be the resignation dates for maintained school classroom teachers.

| Calendar for SLT advertisements | | | |
|---|---|---|---|
| | Headteacher | Deputy Headteacher | Assistant Headteacher |
| September | Very few; some Independent schools for following September in 12 months' time | Very few | Very few |
| October | Medium all month; Independent schools last-ditch advertisements for coming September | First 2 weeks medium, then few. Independent schools advertising for coming September | First 2 weeks medium, then few or very few |
| November | Medium all month | Few | Few or very few |
| December | First 2 weeks medium | Few | Very few |
| January | From mid month very high | From mid month very high, especially Independent schools for September | From mid-month high |
| February | Very high – peak period all month. Independent schools advertising for September in 19 months' time | Very high. Independent schools advertising in particular for coming September | Very high |
| March | Very high peak period to last week, then high. Independent schools advertising for September in 18 months' time | Very high – peak period all month - Independent schools advertising in particular for coming September | Very high – peak period all month |
| April | High, and last week very high. Independent schools advertising for September in 17 months' time | Very high – peak period all month | Very high – peak period all month |
| May | First week very high, then medium – but Independent schools advertising for September in 16 months' time | First two weeks very high – peak period, then low | First two weeks still peak period, then very low |
| June | Medium – but Independent schools advertising for September in 15 months' time | Very few | Very few |
| July | Low, but still some Independent schools advertising for September in 14 months' time | Very few | Very few |

# REFEREES FOR A SLT APPLICATION

E arly in the preparation process, you need to identify your referees. Unless you are already a headteacher, your own headteacher will be the first one; the second could be a former headteacher, (although not from more than 3 years ago), a deputy head if you are currently an assistant head, the headteacher or deputy headteacher at another school where you work collaboratively, or the Chair of Governors.

Those who are already headteachers looking to move to another headship may find it hardest to find two referees. Obviously your first referee will be the Chair of Governors.

Depending on your relationship with him or her, you might like to suggest that it could be helpful if you showed an example of the typical format for a headship reference, and the type of information to include. You then immediately hand over a pre-prepared copy of your own version of the reference you would hope that the Chair of Governors would write for you. You might be lucky and have it accepted in its entirety.

At this level, I think that it is quite appropriate to ask if it might be possible to discuss your reference with both referees. Go in with a sheet of achievements as an aide-mémoire for them.

Your second reference could come from whoever else might be considered your line manager as a headteacher, depending on the type of school. It could be someone in the local authority, or the Academy Trust, perhaps the Diocesan Office. Have you ever worked with a School Improvement Partner or School Effectiveness Advisor? If your school is in a group or trust, it could very well be a fellow headteacher with whom you have worked within the group.

# IDENTIFYING YOUR UNIQUE SELLING POINTS

I have given details of defining these in the earlier section. For a senior leadership post, this is even more important than for a classroom post, and must go even more closely hand-in-hand with a school's BBs. Not just the specific BBs of the actual school that you are going to be applying for, but in general – what are schools looking for in a headteacher? And the next question is, obviously: have you got what it is that schools want?

# CHARACTERISTICS OF SUCCESSFUL SCHOOL LEADERS

T ry a bit of Googling to see what, in general, are considered the characteristics and attributes of a successful school leader. If we sum up what we see, it is that the desirable headteacher is one who is an inspirational and visionary leader, with the ability and determination to improve a school's standards. Those are going to be key criteria for most governing bodies, even if they do not say so explicitly in their person specification, so these should come out in your application.

You may find it helpful before venturing onto the waters of SLT applications to get the views of your colleagues. Not their view of your career prospects, but their view of you as a colleague and person. 360-degree feedback in other words. I would suggest, since you are going forward to a whole-school role, that you invite all your school colleagues to participate. Even those with whom you think that you have no contact may have an assessment of you, garnered from other colleagues, from their students, even from parents. It would be good to have a clear understanding of how others view you. Google *360-degree feedback* for suggestions on how to organise it. Once you have this you can begin to see how to present yourself effectively in your application.

# THE APPLICATION FORM FOR A SENIOR LEADERSHIP POSITION

G enerally these are standard forms, so do read again the advice on application forms above. Sometimes, however, they have a special SLT application form which asks you to answer, at length, specific questions. Almost a written examination! Here are actual examples from various SLT application forms, each leaving a whole page of the form for you to answer their question:

*What is the role of a deputy head?* (Don't they know?!)

*What has been the most difficult decision you have had to take?*

*Describe a situation when you had to introduce a curriculum change against fierce opposition from staff*

*What are your greatest achievements over the last 3 years?*

*Give an example of how you have taken responsibility for improving the quality of people, systems or outputs. Explain the situation, your actions and the outcome*

*Give an example from your present role where you initiated, developed and implemented a marketing exercise or project. How did you measure its success? Quantitative information will help the panel assess your example*

*Give a specific example where you initiated and delivered a project which has generated extra non-fees income for the school. Did the income outweigh the costs incurred? The more specific you can be with quantitative financial data, the easier it will be for the selection panel to assess your experience.*

You might also be asked to answer this sort of questions in a written assessment in the interview. For this type of exercise it can often be helpful to use the STAR approach. This is a mnemonic whereby you couch your answer according to these keywords: Situation, Task, Action, Result. Sometimes you need to modify this slightly:

*Give an example where you have had to introduce a change to working practices which has met resistance or opposition. Briefly set out the proposed change, the opposition encountered and the final solution.*

Here you would tackle it by using not STAR but STRAR: Situation, Task, Resistance, Action, Result. A general comment here is that whenever you are asked to evaluate something that you have done, whether in writing or in the interview, it may be appropriate to consider what you learned from it, and say so.

General advice on a SLT application would be to pay to get it professionally typed. Any application really, but specifically a SLT one, as a professionally set out letter or statement (and executive summary) look so much better than anything that most of us can produce. That all-important first impression.

Many schools have a prospectus for prospective parents; others have a prospectus for prospective headteachers, that is the application pack that they provide for candidates. Both of these are marketing tools, selling the school. Your application, too, is a marketing prospectus, selling you. You must ensure that it is an effective marketing tool.

# EXAMPLES TO AVOID

N ot all senior leadership candidates ensure that their application is an effective marketing tool. I am sure that you would not wish to copy these ineffective extracts from applications. What impression do they give of the candidates?

*I bring operational and strategic management skills, alongside experience in transformation initiatives including school improvement and start-up expertise within organisations*

*I have knowledge and experience of admin and strategic development in school improvement, as well as specialist expertise in managing and inspiring success, achievement in education, developing stakeholder success and introduction of new curricula*

*I actively encourage all pupils to be adaptable to change in a pro-active manner*

*In the role of deputy headteacher I would work closely with my line manager to familiarize myself with any relevant planning. I would use my excellent speaking and listening skills to engage with my colleagues to draw up an action plan for the future. Allied to this would be developing the school's planning working with my fellow SLT members to draw up a timetable of meetings for the term.*

These are mere gobbledy-gook, empty words conveying little meaning, or conveying rubbish, and doing the applicant no favours at all. The final quotation seems to suggest that strategic planning is merely arranging the meetings calendar.

Heaven help us! I repeat here the warning that I gave at the very beginning of this book: non-specialist advisors, that is those not specialising in education, are not a good investment. The candidate above spent several hundred pounds to get these sentences written by a placement agency.

Defining your own USPs so that you can present them in an application and subsequently in an interview is time-consuming; ensure that your statements are honest, and set out clearly your values, your passion and your vision for the role. Because it is these characteristics, and especially your vision, that will be important.

For a headteacher it will be your vision for the school; for other SLT members it will be your vision for the role within the context of that school, what you would set out to achieve, within the overall school vision. Your vision is a key point in a senior leadership application. I could say: your vision and your passion.

# STRUCTURE OF AN EFFECTIVE SENIOR LEADERSHIP APPLICATION LETTER OR STATEMENT

A s with the advice given earlier for teacher applications, your application needs to be very well structured to illustrate your communication skills. It will be your decision whether or not to have headings in the letter or statement; personally, I would leave them in. The shortlisting and interviewing panels will be made up of very busy people, and giving them pointers in this manner is helpful. But even if you decide not to have them in the final version, do use them in the working document, as it will help you ensure that your final version is logically structured and hangs together well.

The headings to use could be taken from their documentation, if they are sensible. This would show clearly that you are on the same wavelength as them. If their documentation is poorly presented and organised, or if their sections are not appropriate for showing you to your best advantage, then use something else. Here is a possibility for you to consider:

*First paragraph without heading: what attracts me is my vision for the future of XXX school*
*The pupil experience*
*Raising achievement*
*Delivering the vision*
*Final paragraph on working with the Governing Body*

N.B. You will need to check their documents to see whether to use pupils or students in your application. And having made the decision, do a final check just before sending off the document by doing a search on the other, non-selected, word, to ensure that you haven't left the wrong one in somewhere. Do it at the same time that you do the search that I recommended earlier to check that you haven't included the name of the wrong school.

Here is another suggested structure:

*Current and recent experience*
*The pupil experience*
*The priorities of your post* (i.e. what you believe that they want/need, your reading of their needs)
*The future of XXX school* (i.e. what you will do in response to known and named, and unknown, national or local initiatives or challenges)

Still undecided about the structure for your application? Try these:

*First paragraph without heading*
*Current and recent experience*
*Culture and ethos of the school*
*Curriculum and teaching*

*Organisational effectiveness*
*Final paragraph possibly without heading*

These middle three are obviously the Domains taken from the *Headteachers' Standards (2020),* always a useful document.

# CONTENT OF AN EFFECTIVE SENIOR LEADERSHIP APPLICATION LETTER OR STATEMENT

T he first section should set out your stall quite clearly. Do not waste any space at all in the letter or statement by some vague reference to your career to date and how you are very keen to join their school. Especially do not say how this post would be good for developing your career! Too many SLT applicants do that, losing the game before they have started. Start strong.

# EXAMPLES

Here are some examples of content of the letter, so you can see what I mean.

> *The challenges that this post offers match the skills and experience that I have acquired in my role as Y at XXX. If appointed, I would expect to use these skills to determine with the Governing Body a strategic vision that would enable us to strengthen the ethos of the school; to raise achievement; to develop the curriculum and ICT-based delivery methods to prepare our pupils for successful progression; to manage the accommodation strategy to support the curriculum and co-curricular activities; to ensure financial stability, and to further promote the reputation of XX school both locally and nationally.*

This first paragraph pushes all the buying buttons that you identified from their documents, and is looking to the future, to what you will do, not back to what you have done.

Of course, it is very easy to make sweeping statements like this, and the panel will wish to investigate this with you in the interview, but here it at least shows that you know what should be done, even if you haven't yet spelled out how you would achieve this. And note the phrase *our pupils*; you are associating yourself with the school from the outset.

My first possible structure had a very early section on the pupil experience. You would be surprised (at least I hope that it would be a surprise!) how many senior leadership applications have little reference to pupils. Make them the centre of your application with something like this:

> *Raising aspirations, encouraging success, promoting excellence, setting high standards, valuing intellectual qualities, celebrating achievement: these are important elements in the ethos of a school.*
>
> *I want the pupils in our care to taste success and thus acquire a taste for it; I want their lives, both academically and personally, to be changed for the better because of the time that they spent with us. I want them in the future to be better undergraduates, better employees, better citizens because of what we gave them.*
>
> *This is a vision that I can turn into reality in XXX School.*

This section puts pupils squarely in a prime position in the application letter, and looks to the future, highlighting your vision, your delivery of the vision. Again, it doesn't say how you will do it – it will be up to you to explain this clearly in the interview.

This example above is quite passionate, almost emotional. If an emotional, passionate statement is not you, then do not force it. It would be counterproductive to do so, because your application must be honest and true to you as the person that you are, not as some person you think that the panel would want you to be.

In all applications, it is crucial that you present an honest picture of yourself, but for headships it's even more so – because some people have been so desperate for a headship that they have portrayed themselves on paper as something that they are not, only to find that the governing body is more than disappointed when faced with the reality of who the new headteacher actually is. Not only can it be career suicide, it has been known to lead to mental health problems for the square peg in the round hole.

You will need a final short section which sums up why they need you by emphasising what you have to offer. Here is an example which is less emotional than some of the previous ones:

> *I recently undertook a personal assessment exercise, part of which included asking over 100 colleagues to assess me (anonymously if they wished) with a list of six adjectives or phrases of their choice that gave a balanced evaluation. My colleagues' judgement is that I am committed to excellence, have high personal standards, am energetic, approachable, supportive and efficient. I believe that these attributes, coupled with my achievements to date, would allow me to make a valuable contribution to the continuing success of XXX school as a centre of excellence in education for the community in XXX and the surrounding area.*

This has come from the 360 degree feedback exercise that I suggested earlier.

Throughout the application letter or statement, make sure that you give *outcomes*, preferably with data to back up. Don't just say what you have done or do, show the impact that you have had and mention occasionally that this fits in with what they are hoping for.

# THE EXECUTIVE SUMMARY FOR A SENIOR LEADERSHIP APPLICATION

An executive summary is, in my view, an important addition to your application. An addition, not a replacement for the statement or letter. Do remind yourself of what I wrote in the section above on executive summaries, and in particular the comments made by people who receive them as part of an application.

For a senior leadership application you may allow yourself to go to two sides if necessary, although just the one is preferable. Here is an example of part of an executive summary.

*Examples*

## *Summary*

## Jane Brown : Applicant for Deputy Headship of Greenfields School

| Your requirements | My experience |
|---|---|
| • Leadership of others | • Assistant Head at Gasworks High<br>• Led team that was awarded top grade in Ofsted Inspection, 2014 |
| • Understanding others | • Investor in People Assessor, April 2014: *"Gasworks staff hold you in high esteem and appreciate you as a supportive and caring Assistant Head"* |
| • Drive for Improvement | • GCSE A*-C rose from 46% to 68% in 3 years under my leadership of Teaching and Learning |
| • Planning and thinking ahead | • Managed operational and strategic planning cycles in Leafy Lane Comprehensive<br>• Contribute to setting and achieving of strategic objectives in Gasworks High |
| • Understanding the School as a Business | • *Successful in-depth experience of*: budget management; financial planning; monitoring of monthly management accounts; efficiency gains through resource management; income generation; managing change; personnel issues; use of management information to support decision-making |
| • Cognitive ability | • High scores in Verbal Reasoning and Numeracy tests |
| • Leadership of School and SMT | • *Contribution to Management Committees*: Senior Leadership Team; Curriculum Management Group; IT Strategy Group; Quality Committee; Academic Board |
| • Staff appointment, training and other staffing matters | • Chaired 8 appointment panels this year<br>• Manage the Performance Management Scheme in Gasworks High |
| • Recruitment and discipline of pupils | • Responsible for 180 new enrolments per year, including links with feeders<br>• Manage all student matters including discipline, recommendation for exclusion and contacts with Social Services |
| • Organisation, policies and procedures | • Chair Curriculum Management Group, the major policy development forum<br>• Devised procedures for: Trips and Visits, Appointments etc. |

Here is another example:

## Summary of Application

### Ravinder Bhogal: Applicant for post of Deputy Head

| Leafy Lane High School's requirements | My experience |
|---|---|
| • Successful middle or senior leadership record | • 4 years as Assistant Head of Grungy Green School<br>• Experience of leading pastoral, curriculum and support teams at both senior and middle level |
| • An appreciation of the needs of a multi ethnic school | • Have worked effectively in 3 multi ethnic schools<br>• An understanding of the ethnic communities and their needs<br>• Ability to communicate in 3 community languages |
| • Confidence in the use of ICT | • Very confident user of all Microsoft packages and SIMS Modules<br>• Effective use of data for tracking and monitoring student performance for raising achievement |
| • Experience in a school with a Sixth form | • Have worked in 3 schools with Sixth forms<br>• Currently manage the Head of Sixth Form<br>• 14 years' experience of successful teaching of A-level |
| • Ability to timetable | • Have good understanding of the principles for timetabling<br>• Am willing to learn! |
| • Effective membership of Senior Leadership Team | • Proven whole-school strategic leadership<br>• Contribute to formulation of whole-school targets<br>• Develop, implement and review policies to achieve targets<br>• Contribute to strategic planning and SDP<br>• Maintain a presence in pupil areas throughout the day<br>• Set and maintain high standards, including personal example<br>• My lead on raising achievement has gained commendation |
| • Learning and Teaching | • Whole-school responsibility for raising attainment and ensuring high-quality pupil learning<br>• Initiatives developed by me have, in 3 years, raised attainment at GCSE A*-C from 54% to 67%, and at A2 from 16% A-B to 39% A*-B<br>• Use of data to monitor student progress and quality of teaching |
| • Leading and managing staff | • Direct leadership and management of XX staff overall<br>• Manage the examinations office and provide timely analysis of results to feed into our strategies for raising attainment<br>• MA in Leadership with thesis on identification, preparation and development of middle leaders for succession |

All executive summaries are best based on the person specification and/or the job description for that specific school, although of course since different schools may well include similar criteria, your evidence will be the same in different summaries. In fact, you may also use the same evidence for two different criteria on the same summary; as long as it is relevant (and good!), that's no problem.

Occasionally there is such a poor specification or description from a school that it is useless for demonstrating that you are a very good candidate. In which case your best bet is to use the characteristics from the *Headteachers' Standards (2020)*. That's tricky because not only are there a lot of them, but they are very wordy. Cutting them down to size by prioritising, condensing and combining, as I advise in the earlier section on executive summaries, is not going to be easy.

One final word on executive summaries. Your evidence has to be good. I have known Governors to be very impressed by a beautifully presented summary, until I, in my role as consultant, have pointed out that the actual evidence was rubbish. If your evidence is not strong, then perhaps this is not the right job for you.

# 16. APPLYING FOR A TEACHING JOB FROM A POTENTIAL POSITION OF WEAKNESS

T he best position to be in when applying for a teaching job is in employment, in a school in the United Kingdom, where you have been working successfully for two years at least. But not everybody is in that lucky position. So what do you do in other circumstances?

The advice here is firstly to be open about it; don't try to hide it. Secondly, don't go into enormous detail, just be brief. And thirdly think through what could be the positives of your situation, and present those clearly. There may not always be these positives, but often there are.

# WANTING TO MOVE ON AFTER A SHORT TIME

L et us suppose that you are applying for another post after just a term or two in a school (you have spoken to your current headteacher about this, haven't you?), don't just apply and not mention it. You need to acknowledge in the application that you are hoping to move on fast, and give a brief reason.

Ensure that it is not a reason that speaks negatively about your current school; don't even say *It's the wrong school for me*, turn it round and say *I realise that I made a mistake in joining XXX school, as I am not the right teacher for this school. I believe, however, that my attributes of X, Y and Z would enable me to make a positive contribution to Z school.*

This is a very important point. To put it bluntly, a school wants pilgrims, not refugees. It wants to be sought out and be loved for itself, not to be seen as just anywhere to escape to.

If you are lucky, you will have a practical reason for wishing to move. Need to be nearer family or partner, unreliable transport, or commuting taking more out of you than you expected.

# DOING SUPPLY TEACHING

T hat to me, as someone involved in appointing staff, is not necessarily a disadvantage, but it is up to you to present this positively in an application so that the shortlisting panel can appreciate all that you could bring to their school.

Can you identify what you have gained from doing supply teaching? I reckon that it has given you resourcefulness and versatility, enabled you to observe a variety of different classroom practices and learn from them, improved your classroom management skills from dealing with a wide range of different pupils, from the too-compliant to the downright difficult. You have gained self-reliance, have learnt to work co-operatively with colleagues in different types of schools, you are able to deal with difficult situations (and difficult people), you have experience of a wide range of year groups and can use different types of electronic teaching aids. You are very flexible in your attitude towards your job and can adapt easily to new situations, new requirements, and new examination specifications. You have become a much more effective teacher and a better colleague than you were before, and are very grateful for these opportunities.

Are you setting all this out in your statement or letter, right at the beginning, getting it all in before you even mention the word "Supply"?

*Since successfully completing my PGCE in* (insert here the date) *I have been able to acquire* (insert here the attributes you have decided on) *through a series of contracts as a supply teacher in schools including* (insert here the names of one or two well-known and well-respected schools)

It is possible to write a whole paragraph on the benefits of supply, what you have gained through it, and what it will therefore enable you to bring to this school.

It can be very helpful to get someone for whom you've worked recently in a school to write one of your references. It could even be a parallel class teacher, if you have a headteacher as another referee. If possible, ask if they would include the phrase "*Would appoint without hesitation if I had a vacancy*". It would also be helpful to include in your statement or letter that schools asked for you by name from the agency (but only if true, not if not!), and that you had repeat visits to schools because you were a valued colleague.

I'll just remind you of something that I said earlier, when talking about identifying your referees. Do try to avoid using an agency as a main referee, as their references can be somewhat minimalist. Try to use two school-based referees if you possibly can. I suggest that in one sentence in your letter or statement, you give the name and contact of your supply agency, saying that the school may wish to contact them for further details. That gets over the issue that an agency can sometimes be considered a current employer, and thus you must give it as a referee.

Overall, don't be apologetic, supply is great preparation for the day-to-day of teaching.

# RETURNING TO TEACHING

A re you returning to teaching after an absence? You might be, for example, a parent who has been involved full time in childcare and now hoping to return to the classroom, or someone who left teaching for another career and is now regretting it. Here the issue may well be that you are out of touch with current classroom and school practice. A term's worth of supply teaching could overcome this, so that should be your first port of call if possible, although your financial situation may not allow this.

For primary teachers, this experience gap can sometimes also be resolved by doing voluntary work for a few days a week as a TA – or indeed getting a job as a TA – for a term or so. This would have the advantage of providing you with an up-to-date reference.

A secondary teacher might try doing examination marking, or examination tutoring, to show familiarity with the current specifications. In either case, do read the advice above about supply teaching, and see how it could be relevant for you.

What have you gained from your time spent out of the classroom, whether with your children or in a different job? How would this translate into a new job as a teacher in a school?

The Department for Education has a dedicated section on Return to Teaching. In particular, it provides a wide-ranging package of support for returners; check it out. It is a good idea to register with them and investigate the general information on returning, with resources for getting up-to-date with changes in schools including changes to the national curriculum and qualifications, and some downloadable documents with the current behaviour management guidelines.

# RETURNING AFTER WORKING IN A SCHOOL ABROAD

T here are several thousand, several tens of thousands probably, British teachers working in schools abroad who would wish at some stage to return to teaching in the UK. And it can be done. In fact it is done, as every year British teachers return with a suntan and wallets full of banknotes that they can't spend here.

There are some areas and some stages and subjects where there is a shortage of trained and experienced teachers, notably mathematics, English, science, modern languages. Teachers in these subjects will find it easier, and those in other subjects willing to work in large cities too, but there are still hoops to go through and hurdles to jump.

For those of you returning to the UK, there are two major stumbling blocks: *the geography and the history* of your recent career.

The geography refers to being distant from a school here for interviews. UK-based candidates can jump into their car at little notice, but you may find it more difficult to do this, especially if you are in the Far East or south of the equator.

Don't hang your hopes, (as during the covid pandemia)

on having an interview by FaceTime or Skype, even though you got your job in the Bahamas that way, as the statutory guidance to maintained schools in England and Wales has always been that a *face-to-face interview that explores the candidate's suitability to work with children as well as his/her suitability for the post* should take place, for safeguarding reasons. However, during the Covid-19 pandemic, schools were forced to use distance interviews and many have continued with this, so this may be a winner for you. There is a section on video interviews in the companion book ***Interview for a teaching job.***

The following paragraphs refer, therefore, to face-to-face interviews.

You may find that a few Independent schools or academies, even free schools, have always had a different view on this, and been happy with Skype or Zoom interviews, but many won't, partly because they want to see you teaching. Here you will most probably be told that a video of you teaching in your school abroad would not be a suitable alternative, as they want to see you interacting – or actually coping - with their own pupils.

This means that in general to get a position in a school in the UK, you need to come to interview; many of you will find that your school abroad will not be happy for you to be absent for three or four days to make that possible.

A UK interview can also be expensive for you, as with the honourable exception of senior leadership positions (and even then, in these days of budgetary constraints, many state schools will pay expenses only from 'port of entry to UK'), you have very little chance of getting your travel expenses paid from abroad.

Nowadays, in fact, schools in England often no longer pay travel expenses for candidates coming to interview from Manchester or Maidenhead. They are even less likely to pay for you to come from Madrid or Muscat. At best, you might get the train fare from the airport, with no accommodation costs.

A further obstacle could be that a school may even be unwilling to ask you to pay the airfare to come, and so decide not to interview you at all, just rejecting your application out of hand. If you are teaching in Europe, you could pre-empt this by saying in your application that you are planning a visit to the UK shortly, and could arrange it to fit their interview date.

This way, you pay the fare, but the school doesn't feel bad about it. You are out of pocket, but at least you get the chance of an interview. Some schools will pay the airfare and accommodation for the successful candidate, but including it with the first pay packet.

Your recent career history could be the other impediment to appointment.

Just as they can on occasion be somewhat suspicious of applicants from independent schools, some maintained schools and academies can look with a jaundiced eye on applicants from British schools abroad, believing that you have had a pleasant time with model pupils sitting in disciplined rows, bright-eyed, bushy-tailed, and eager to hand in all their homework. To be honest, they could have a point there, couldn't they? I've seen these pupils myself, having been a consultant on Headship applications in Europe, so potential concerns about classroom management need to be addressed in your application.

The other area where your recent career history could a disadvantage is because of the amount of change in education in the UK over the last few years. Things have moved on extremely fast, with new initiatives in learning coming every month, it sometimes seems; you may be considered not to be aware of the pedagogy flavour of the month. You will need to highlight in your application that you teach the UK curriculum, your pupils are successful in GCSE, A-level or the iGCSE and IB, and that you are always very keen to keep up to date, as is shown by (whatever you do in your school for CPD).

Can you take out a digital subscription to the TES, so that you get the magazine delivered to your computer each week? It's full of education news and articles that give handy tips. You might also get just what you need to shine in your interview.

What all this means is that you are possibly unlikely to get a post while you are still abroad. Is it by no means an impossible task, as some people most certainly do manage it, but it is nonetheless not 100% likely that you will get a job so that you can just return in July to Cardiff or Colchester, have your fortnight in a caravan at Torquay or Teignmouth, then start teaching in a school in September. You might well be able to do it, especially if you are based in Europe, but it's best not to base your return on this with no Plan B.

If your school term abroad ends very early in the summer, you could start applying for posts that are advertised after the 31st May resignation deadline; these posts can only be filled by those not currently in permanent posts that are subject to resignation dates: NQTs, unemployed teachers, those on short-term or maternity contracts, and people working abroad. These posts will typically interview from mid-June to mid-July, and you might be able to get back for that. Ensure that you make this clear in your application.

Teachers working abroad sometimes plan to come back, look for a job for a January start, and survive on supply before then. This is not necessarily a good plan. Firstly, there are fewer jobs advertised for January. But above all, supply teaching is less secure than it was, many teachers finding that they get only two or three days a month, especially in the autumn term. Someone offering to teach English, physics or mathematics will find it a lot easier to get supply, however.

Another issue is that you will need some sort of police certificate from your current country of residence if you have been out of the UK for over a year. Ask colleagues at your school abroad what you should get, as different countries have different systems. You are looking for something that says that you are an upright citizen, with no police record. Start asking now about how to get that but don't actually apply for it yet as it could be rejected as being out of date by a very particular school or local authority.

To round off this section, let us consider what you are likely to be paid on your return. You did four years in the UK after your NQT induction year, have since done 5 years abroad working in a British school where you were teaching the National Curriculum, with great results at GCSE and A-level. Surely, they should be offering you M6 on your return, with a jump to the Upper Pay Scale soon? Unfortunately not.

Even under the old system (i.e. up to 1 September 2013), only years teaching in a maintained school in England & Wales or elsewhere in the European Union, employed directly and not via an agency, counted for pay progression. Therefore, your years abroad in a private school never counted for progression up the scale, although some schools – quite a number in fact - did allow it.

The system for paying teachers has now changed, and there are no official scale points (despite the teaching unions advertising them on their websites), no automatic pay rises each year, and certainly no pay portability – by which I mean that the pay scale point in one school used to be carried – portered – to the next school. For several years now, teachers in schools in England and Wales, when they take a new job, have no right to have their current salary maintained, yet alone automatically move up in the new post. Here is some information on this from the NEU:

> *(The government) has ended fixed national pay scale points, extended performance related pay (PRP), removed pay portability and implemented school-based pay determination.*

*The national pay scales, setting out the year-on-year pay progression that teachers can expect, have been replaced by a structure which only sets minimum and maximum rates that schools can pay their staff. Graduates considering teaching no longer have any certainty about pay; teachers in service may find themselves facing slower pay progression than before.*
*All pay progression is now linked to performance. The NEU has always opposed PRP in teaching. The new stronger links to performance and individualised pay decisions are already causing more problems for teachers.*

*The removal of pay portability means that teachers are no longer entitled to keep the progression they have earned through experience. When they move schools they now have to renegotiate their pay. Many tell us they are now less likely to consider moving schools as a result. Teachers on career breaks - mainly women – are likely to be hit hardest of all as they try to re-enter teaching.*

N.B. this extract above refers to pay scales. They no longer exist. The teaching unions got together and took the decision that they would ignore the government's decision to replace the pay scales with pay ranges. So each year they invent the non-existent pay points in the non-existent pay scales. There is no longer a M1 or a M6, whatever they say.

I will add that teachers trying to re-enter the UK teaching market could be similarly hard hit. A school will offer a teacher the minimum that they can to ensure that the teacher accepts the job offer. If there are six candidates shortlisted, four of whom are low on the pay range, then they may offer only a low salary to the successful candidate, knowing that Plan B will get the job filled at that salary if Plan A turns it down.

There is a website run by the government called *Return to teaching in England from Overseas* which may be of help in general.

# APPLYING WITH
# A RECORD OF ILL
# HEALTH ABSENCES

T eachers hoping to return to teaching after a period of ill-health, those currently employed who have an on-going health issue, or indeed those who have had a number of unrelated and minor health problems over the last year or two which overall have added up to quite a few sickness-related absences, may be concerned about applying for jobs. To these we may add the all-too-common situation of a colleague who has suffered – or is still suffering – from work-related stress, depression or anxiety. Will all this be held against you?

There may be a section of the application form which asks how many days absence as a teacher the applicant has had in the past year, or even past two or three years. Even if there isn't, an applicant may fear that there is a similar question asked of referees, or be very aware that their ill-health record in their current or most recent school may well be mentioned in the reference.

This is all a very tricky area, because there are two conflicting pieces of legislation here, as we shall see.

Many claim that it is unlawful to ask for medical information as part of the application, including asking referees. They say that this is made clear in the Equality Act 2010. Others point out that the Equality Act comes head-to-head with the school's obligation to ensure *Fitness to Teach* ... I said at the time (2010) that this would cause problems, and I was right!

A school, i.e. the headteacher, has a legal obligation to ensure *Fitness to teach*. It can thus be said that establishing an applicant's fitness to teach is an intrinsic part of the job and therefore falls within one of the prescribed exceptions to the Equality Act. Most schools do an after-offer medical form, and the offer is subject to a satisfactory medical report.

Many also ask before appointment for details of absences from the referees and sometimes from applicants themselves. Is this legal? Can you refuse to provide this information and still be appointed?

What is the answer here to the conflict between *Fitness to Teach* and *The Equality Act 2010*? I am not a legal employment specialist, so cannot give any answer. A lawyer employed by ATL has said in a document published on their website:

> However, to say that asking questions about an employee's health at the recruitment stage is unlawful is not strictly true as there are a number of exceptions to the rule. For example, questions asked with the intention of establishing whether there is a need to make reasonable adjustments, for the purposes of monitoring diversity, and establishing whether an applicant will be able to carry out a function that is intrinsic to the job, will be permitted.

She went on to say:

> employers may argue that establishing an individual's fitness to teach is an intrinsic part of the job and therefore falls within one of the prescribed exceptions.

However, there has apparently been an about-turn on this, as the document has now been removed from the ATL website.

However *Keeping children safe in education (2022), Statutory guidance for schools and colleges* is very clear:

> *All schools and colleges must . . . verify the candidate's mental and physical fitness to carry out their work responsibilities. A job applicant can be asked relevant questions about disability and health in order to establish whether they have the physical and mental capacity for the specific role*

Conflicting advice makes it difficult for applicants. My advice is that you should be open without going into any great detail. You should certainly answer honestly any question that you are asked. If, for example, there is a question on the application form about whether you are covered by the Equality Act, and your illness or disability is such that you are, then of course you tick YES, but there is no need to go into details.

Similarly, when you get called for interview you tell them if any adjustments need to be made, but until then, why mention it if it is not relevant to your ability to carry out the job to the required standard?

The greater problem comes when your illness or disability is not covered by the Equality Act, and you have had some considerable ill-health absences that will almost certainly be mentioned in any reference. I always suggest mentioning this briefly in your actual letter. You should bring it right out into the open then dismiss it with a reassuring comment. The school wishes to be reassured that you are, indeed, fit to teach.

So my suggestion is that you include towards the end of your letter or statement just a brief sentence mentioning your health almost in passing. Don't make a big deal out of it. Here are some examples of the sort of thing that you might say.

> *I have always had an excellent attendance record until XXX (year) when I had an unexpected health issue for which I was*

*operated on successfully. I am now fully recovered, and there is no impact at all on my professional or personal life, as is shown by the fact that . . .(give some good example of a success).*

Or:

*I feel that I am possibly more able than some to cope with the normal stresses of a teacher's life, having had a period of absence during which I developed coping strategies to enable me to return to work and carry out my role fully, including. . . (give some good example of an achievement).*

Or:

*Having successfully overcome a mild case of anxiety and depression, I am now not only 100% fit but also much better equipped to deal with the stresses of everyday life as a teacher, since my coping strategies work so well. I have in fact recently . . .*

Or again:

*Having successfully gone through a period of ill-health through depression, I have developed coping strategies that mean that I am now much more able to cope with the everyday stresses of teaching as a career. I feel that the experience has strengthened me, enabling me to . . .*

Yet another suggestion:

*Following a brief period of ill-health (from which I am now fully recovered) I am keen to join a school where I can give a long-term commitment to the success of pupils through both my teaching and my contribution to the wider school community and its activities.*

That is my advice: mention it briefly, dismiss it. But you should only do this if you feel comfortable with it, and of course anything you say should always actually be truthful. I think that having this type of brief statement in the letter will pre-empt any concerns that they might have if your reference speaks of a long absence.

# GETTING A NEW JOB AFTER REDUNDANCY

With school budgets being squeezed more and more, especially with increased fuel bills, being made redundant is becoming more common; it should not be a disadvantage when seeking a new post, as there are no negative connotations. State quite clearly in your application that your role is being or has been made redundant; however, do not give the impression that you are desperate and applying for any and every post.

You must still ensure that you show a school that you are applying specifically to them, that their school attracts you because you believe that you could make a positive contribution to it. Re-read all my comments above about the letter or statement and summary. Remember: a school wants pilgrims, not refugees, as I pointed out above; it doesn't wish to be considered just any old port in a storm.

A redundancy gives you certain rights when looking for another job. Your employer, in this case the headteacher, has to give you "reasonable" time off to look for work or to retrain when you are under notice of redundancy and to pay you as normal for this time. Unfortunately, the law does not precisely define what "reasonable" means here, so is therefore a somewhat grey area which can occasionally give rise to disputes.

The legal situation is that you can get full pay for the

equivalent of two fifths of a normal week's pay, even if you are absent for longer than that. Many schools, however, will not put any limit on the number of paid absences for job interviews that they allow you.

This is an advantage as otherwise, although usually you are allowed to go to interview, there is no absolute right, and the headteacher could refuse to let you go. But during your redundancy notice period, you can always go, as long as you have been employed continuously for two years. Your right to time off is not limited to attending interviews, however. You could also ask for time off to arrange new training for yourself.

So good news there, but on the other hand there may be a problem with redundancy.

As you know, assuming that you qualify, you will receive redundancy pay. This is to compensate you for being unemployed. It can be quite a nice sum. You are normally entitled to statutory redundancy pay if you are a direct employee (not employed through an agency) and have been working for your current employer for two years or more. If so, you get half a week's pay for each full year with the employer that you were under 22, one week's pay for each full year you were 22 or older, but under 41, and one and half week's pay for each full year you were 41 or older (Summer 2022 figures).

This sum is not unlimited, however, as you can only claim a maximum of 20 years, and the maximum statutory redundancy receivable is £17,130 in 2022. If you are fortunate, you may have a contract or agreement that allocates more than statutory redundancy, especially in the independent school sector.

So what is the problem? Some local authorities or other teaching employers can include, as a condition for receiving this money, a clause that says something like this: *The redundancy payment will only be made where the employee has been unemployed for a minimum of 30 days continuously from the end of the contract.*

To put it bluntly: you cannot be made redundant at the end of August and then begin at another school on 1$^{st}$ September and retain your redundancy payment.

This is not always the case, but it is sometimes, so you need to check that out once the redundancy process begins, and consult your union. The best situation would be where your current school agrees to terminate your contract and make you redundant on 31 July, thus allowing you to apply for jobs beginning in September. You will have no salary for August, but will collect your redundancy pay and have a much greater chance of getting another job on 1$^{st}$ September than in January, when there are fewer vacancies.

# GETTING A NEW JOB WITH A SETTLEMENT AGREEMENT

For some colleagues, the only way out of a difficult situation in a school is through a settlement agreement (formerly called a compromise agreement). If this is a possibility for you, and you are hoping to continue a career in teaching, I will give one very important piece of advice: **do not accept** any termination date that is not the normal ending date of a teacher's contract, that is to say December 31, April 30 or August 31.

This is absolutely essential. Unfortunately, in my experience of answering queries on the TES online teachers' forum, unions are often not pointing this out to their members. You need not be in school until then (or even until the end of term), but you should be officially in their employment as a teacher. A leaving date other than these will raise a warning flag to a school receiving your application. You may need to give up some of the financial payment in order to cover salary and on-costs for this period, but do so, as it will be worth it in the long run.

It is not going to be all plain sailing to get another job when you have been through capability procedures, or threatened with them; for a start, your self-confidence will be very low. However, it is possible, as I know teachers who have left a school with a settlement agreement, often where they were suffering from work-related stress or even bullying, and gone on to be happy in another permanent teaching post. So take heart from that!

Settlement agreements are confidential, and usually they include a clause stating that neither side will say that the employment was terminated via a settlement agreement. So the first problem is if the application form asks for a reason for leaving. You are going to have to put something in there which is not dishonest but does not mention the agreement.

I consider it best **not** to write *Seeking new challenges*, as to many headteachers this suggests that you jumped before you were pushed, or even that you were pushed. The earlier section on what to give as a reason for leaving discusses this.

Your reason must be honest if vague, and above all must be consistent with what your referees will say; it will flag up a warning for any prospective employer if what you say on your application form is completely different from what your current employer says. Note that consistent with does not mean exactly the same as, just that it does not contradict it.

When you are negotiating with the help of your union the settlement agreement, part of it will include an agreed reference; this issue of reason for leaving should be covered in it, as I explain below. Please also remember that even with a settlement agreement, which usually means that you were not on the best of terms with your headteacher when you left, you should still follow the rule that your current or most recent headteacher is your first referee. Anything else will look fishy as it is contrary to requirements.

A final and possibly negative point. There was a regulation introduced a while ago, in September 2012, that if a prospective new employer asks the previous employer if there has been any formal capability proceedings in the previous two years, then the previous employer must say so and give details.

That's irrespective of what the settlement agreement says about agreed references and not revealing that a settlement agreement exists. An agreed reference in a settlement agreement cannot prevent formal capability being disclosed if there is a specific question about it.

# GETTING A NEW JOB WITH AN AGREED REFERENCE

**W**hile negotiating the settlement agreement, especial care should be taken over the agreed reference. I suggest that you do your very best to have the points I outline below included in the agreement and reference. Your union should be the one working for you on this, but some are less thorough than others, so get prepared yourself.

The first thing that you need to know about an agreed reference is that it has to be agreed. Therefore both you and the school have to agree to the wording. This means that if you don't like what they say, and you have evidence to show that it should not be there, or have evidence to prove that there are other positive points that could be included, then you say so.

Don't ignore that *evidence* bit.

You can't just have any old thing included because you fancy it. An agreed reference has to follow the rules of other references. The legal requirement is for a reference to be fair and factually accurate. If, because of negligent misstatement (inclusion of inaccurate or omission of important information), you suffer detriment (loss), you may claim damages. So the headteacher will be keen to get the reference right, just as you are keen to have a fair reflection of your skills, abilities and contribution to the school.

If you have been following my advice right from the beginning of the book, you will have set up some files that will help you with the evidence needed. So flick through the folders – in particular your Professional development, Performance management, Pupil outcomes and Trumpet file – to pull out the evidence that you will quote when requesting amendments to the first version of the agreed reference. Or even to hand in as a neat bullet point list of points to include before the reference gets written. Remember though – you will need evidence.

So what sort of thing should be included in an agreed reference? Check the school's version to see if it includes these points as a minimum.

1. Firstly and above all you need a safeguarding statement to be in there. Usually put at the end

2. Something about successful teaching, with data if available, and any observation comments

3. If Performance Management came up with some good quotes or an overall favourable outcome, include this

4. And something about good professional relationships with pupils including any pastoral role – were you a form tutor?

5. Teamwork and working co-operatively with colleagues. Talk about producing materials to share

6. Good communication with parents and carers

7. Contribution to the wider school clubs, trips etc

8. Supporting the school ethos, especially for subsequent applications to faith schools where this will be important

Think about all those suggestions - some more ideas may

pop into your mind. Think of evidence for all of them - how would you prove it? Provide the evidence to your headteacher before the reference gets written.

Obviously, the reference has to be honest and truthful, so if any of my suggestions do not accurately reflect your time in the school, they cannot be included.

Child Protection is going to be an important aspect of the agreed reference, and it should conclude with a statement similar to this:

> *I can confirm that **(name)** has not been the subject of disciplinary proceedings (whether formal or informal) involving issues related to the safety and welfare of children or young people. I can further confirm that no allegations or concerns have been raised (whether formally or informally) about **(him/her)** which relate to the safety and welfare of children or young people.*

Clearly this can only be included if it is true; the brutal truth is that if it is not true, then you may have serious difficulties in getting another position working in a school at any level, so you should discuss this with your union.

There are also the dreaded tick box or pro-forma references. No agreed reference can cover all eventualities, and pro-forma references come with so many different questions that they would seem to foil the concept of any agreement over the reference.

That's why it is important that your settlement agreement comes with a statement similar to this:

> *The Employer agrees to provide the Employee with the reference as agreed, and when responding to a written or telephone request for a reference from a prospective employer, including a pro-forma reference, will do so in a manner which*

*is consistent with the agreed reference and not more negative in any way including by omission.*

The major point that really makes pro-forma references dreaded is that they usually include something along the lines of: *Would you employ this person again?* There is, I'm afraid, nothing that you can do about this question, except cross your fingers, as you cannot expect the headteacher to reply dishonestly to this.

I also suggest that you agree with the headteacher, and ensure that it is included in the settlement agreement, what will be given as the reason for leaving. See my earlier section when I discuss reasons for leaving as part of the application form.

Then we come to telephone references. A prospective employer can not only phone up a past employer, whether or not you have given them as a referee, but is encouraged to do so by the statutory guidance if there are any concerns or queries. You cannot control what is said by anyone who is not writing an agreed reference, but the statement that I have suggested above should mitigate the chances of a negative reference being given over the phone by your first referee.

Is it a good strategy, therefore, to avoid an agreed reference and use instead an open reference or testimonial, one that begins *To whom it may concern*?

Most certainly not, as these are not worth the paper that they are written on. Employers are generally advised to ignore them entirely as they cannot be relied on. Was it written by a friend of yours on some fancy headed paper designed to deceive? A school cannot run the risk of accepting these.

Another question often asked is will they know that it's an agreed reference?

I'm afraid that the answer is yes, quite probably they will. People like me can usually spot them. And, indeed, some reference forms include a sentence similar to this just above the place to sign:

> *I confirm that this reference is given freely and is not an agreed reference as part of a settlement agreement or any other mutual agreement.*

But will a school automatically reject you because of an agreed reference? I obviously cannot speak here for every school and every headteacher. But let's just remember the basics: a reference must be fair and factually accurate. So even if it's agreed, a reference should be showing what you have done and how you did it. This means that headteachers, even suspecting or knowing that it's agreed, can still rely on the reference. By the time they get the reference, the employer is committed to seeing you at interview, so will use their own judgment too.

An agreed reference, even if recognised as such, may not be a problem. Many teachers have been able to get permanent posts with such references.

# GETTING A NEW JOB WITH A CRIMINAL RECORD OR A DISQUALIFICATION UNDER THE CHILDCARE ACT

T his, as you can imagine, is a more difficult situation, especially as it includes a teacher being disqualified through no fault or action of their own, as they could be *Disqualified by association*, due to other people in their household, as defined in the document *Disqualification under the Childcare Act 2006 Statutory guidance for local authorities, maintained schools, academies and free schools, Updated August 2018*.

What this means is that a teacher would be disqualified to teach or take care of children under the age of 8 if there is living or employed in their household anyone who has committed certain violent and sexual criminal offences against children and adults. If you believe that you fall into this category, you must consult the document above and your union.

If you yourself have committed any violent and sexual criminal offences against children or adults, including a spouse, you may be disqualified from working in a school with any age group. I cannot give advice on this, and you should consult your union.

My advice is that a criminal record for other offences should be declared on application by enclosing (if making a hard-copy application) or sending separately to the school (if making an electronic application) a sealed envelope for the attention of the headteacher, marked Private and Confidential. In this you identify yourself and the job for which you are applying, set out the conviction, including the circumstances and the date and, if relevant, your age at the time. Make it brief and factual, but do, at the end, mitigate it if possible by pointing out that it was a youthful indiscretion that you have learnt from, and that you have subsequently not re-offended.

You may even wish to consider adding that this youthful experience of the judiciary can make you a more effective form tutor at secondary level, as although you would never share this information about yourself with other staff or students, it does help you see the warning signs of potential wrong-doing and thus take steps to turn the students round.

Many application forms have a question about offending, and require you to provide the details as I have just described. My advice is that even if the form does not tell you to do this, you should do it anyway. The offence will be discovered by the school when they do the appropriate checks on you as the successful candidate, and at that stage could cause the school to withdraw their offer in a knee-jerk reaction, whereas if they had had time to consider it before shortlisting you, they could perhaps understand and accept that this was a one-off. The sealed letter gives you a chance to put your case up front.

Most schools have a policy on the recruitment of ex-offenders. I suggest Googling this to see what a typical policy is.

Within such a policy, I would expect the headteacher and Governing Body to consider a number of factors, including the type of offence (for example, a conviction for uncontrolled rages leading to violence would pose a threat to the school community), the likelihood of re-offending, the impact on the school community of any such re-offending, and also, without re-offending, if the information about the record were to become public, whether this would bring the school into disrepute or cause the staff, students or parents to lose their confidence in the school. In any of those circumstances then a headteacher is likely to choose not to interview a candidate.

Enclosing an explanatory letter with your application is the best step forward since you cannot now turn the clock back.

N.B. *Keeping children safe in education 2022 Statutory guidance for schools and colleges* includes the following:

*Shortlisted candidates should be asked to complete a self-declaration of their criminal record or information that would make them unsuitable to work with children. Self-declaration is subject to Ministry of Justice guidance on the disclosure of criminal records, further information can be found on GOV.UK*

*For example:*

*· if they have a criminal history*

*· if they are included on the children's barred list*

*· if they are prohibited from teaching*

*· if they are prohibited from taking part in the management of an independent school*

*· information about any criminal offences committed in any country in line with the law as applicable in England and Wales, not the law in their country of origin or where they were convicted*

*• if they are known to the police and children's local authority social care*

*• if they have been disqualified from providing childcare (see paras 262-266), and,*

*• any relevant overseas information.*

# 17. THE NEXT STEP

Once you have sent off the application you should begin preparing for the interview; don't wait until you actually are called in to begin your preparation, as you might not have time. I know of one example of someone who was sent an e-mail in the early hours of the morning for an interview that very same day. Obviously a last-minute replacement for a candidate who had pulled out. And the last-minute replacement got the job.

*My* next step was to write the book telling you how to be successful in your interview; it is now available on Amazon Kindle: ***Interview for a Teaching Job.***

I'd like to remind you to go back to the beginning and re-read that sample letter from a website. Can you now see what is wrong with it?

The next page gives you the answers to this, but do go first and read the letter again.

An example letter not to copy

# 18. SPOILER ALERT: COMMENTS ON THE POOR EXAMPLE LETTER AT BEGINNING OF BOOK

S ome of the reasons why you should not use this letter as a model:

Too short

Grammar errors

Punctuation errors

Varied spelling with US and UK usage in the same sentence

Repetition of *I feel*, which is in every paragraph but one

Every paragraph begins with the word I

Trite comments

Generalisations made with no supporting evidence

Ridiculous statements springing from use of jargon: *meeting needs by having an in-depth understanding of needs*

We are told that the job would suit the applicant perfectly as a major reason for the appointment

The second reason for appointing her is that s/he is familiar to (sic) the area

Nowhere do we learn what the candidate would bring to the school, how the school would benefit from this appointment

We learn nothing about the candidate, except that s/he works locally and has been teaching for four years

Does not name current school

Does not provide references

And the letter ends by confidently expecting to be telephoned for an interview.

# EPILOGUE

May your application be successful in getting the position that you hope for to begin, or continue, in this wonderful profession of teaching.

# AFTERWORD

If you have found this book to be useful, please do give it a brief review on its Amazon page. Thank you.

If you have spotted typos or other errors, please send me a Direct Message via Twitter @Theo_Griff . My account is open to receive DMs.

# ABOUT THE AUTHOR

## Theo Griff

Theo Griff has several decades of experience as a middle and senior leader in a range of education establishments: state schools, independent schools, tertiary college, sixth-form college and university, and has worked as a consultant on staff appointments to both schools and teacher and leadership recruitment agencies, both in the UK and abroad.

For nearly twelve years, she was also the forum host on the popular TES advice forum for teachers, answering thousands of queries for jobseekers and helping them get jobs – and promotions - teaching in schools in the UK and in British schools abroad.

The weekend seminars that she ran in the TES building in London had extremely positive reviews from participants, as did the one-to-one career consultations.

For several years she contributed articles and a regular column on employment in schools to the weekly TES magazine.

# PRAISE FOR AUTHOR

1. *New applicants for teaching posts have a clear guide in simple steps and with sound underlying principles on how to make their applications work effectively for them. And not only teaching posts, but also for positions of responsibility and senior leadership posts with an added bonus of sound guidance of how to dig yourself out of the redundancy pit.*

2. *Succinct, clear and relevant. Having lead, and sat on, many recruitment panels, I think that Theo's advice is extremely useful to anyone applying for a job in education, including teaching assistants.*

3. *A must read for anyone aspiring to the next level up in the career. Theo gives insightful, concise, and practical advice on how to really make you stand out from other candidates. I have 12 years of teaching experience but this book has changed my viewpoint on making a great application.*

4. *A brilliant book, read in conjunction with Interview for a teaching job which is equally as good. Full of good sound advice. A must read for all .*

5. *I've been following TheoGriff for years on the TES forums and the book is in keeping with her usual firm but fair advice. It's easy to read and informative and it's made me really excited about returning to*

*teaching. I'm looking forward to buying the next book to get all the useful advice I will need for interviews!*

*6. Whether you are a Beginning Teacher looking to get onto that all-important first rung of your teaching career ladder, or an aspiring Head, this pithy and practical book will help you to avoid the common pitfalls of applications, and coach you into identifying how you can press the selection panel's "buttons" to secure an interview. I found particularly useful the reflections on identifying your own USPs as a candidate and using them to match yourself to the kinds of schools to apply for. The advice on tailoring your personal statement (writing them is a dark art!) to the candidate brief is insightful and does some genuine myth-busting.*

*7. Excellent coverage of the key areas and skills needed by teachers for successful job hunting . Clearly explains the pitfalls and problems with standard and ill thought through applications .As a recruitment specialist I recommend this is on the standard reading for all new teachers.*

*8. This is a sensible, straightforward book that gives great advice no teacher applying for a job can afford to be without. Whatever your desired next step in teaching, from NQT to headship, this book has something for you.*

*- EXTRACTS FROM REVIEWS ON THE AMAZON WEBSITE*

# TEACHING JOB SERIES
# BY THEO GRIFF

The aim of this series is to support teachers to get jobs at all levels from NQT to Headteacher through pertinent and practical advice on applications and interviews.

The books relate to teaching posts in England and Wales, mainly in schools but also in colleges. However, much of the advice will also be relevant to jobseekers in other educational establishments, both in the United Kingdom and overseas.

## Applying For A Teaching Job

During her time in school leadership and consultancy, Theo Griff has read thousands of applications for both classroom teaching and leadership posts, and rejected 80% of them based on the application weaknesses that she will reveal here.

In this book she is now sharing with you the secrets to success when applying for a teaching job.

Whether you are a NQT about to apply for the very first time for the job to start your career, an experienced teacher looking to move into middle leadership, or aiming for the top as a member of a senior leadership team, this book will support you throughout the application process.

Full of brand-new up-to-date tips and suggestions, this essential guide is comprehensive and thorough; it gives specific advice that makes you take a fresh look at how to write an application.

Applying for a teaching job is the practical guide that will show you step-by-step how to draft an application that effectively presents who you are, what you stand for, what you have to offer a school, and why they should appoint you.

You will see the exact techniques used by successful candidates to persuade the shortlisting committee to invite them for interview.

You will get the key to making sure that your application stands out from the crowd for all the right reasons.

## Interview For A Teaching Job

During her years in leadership and consultancy, Theo Griff has interviewed around a thousand candidates for teaching and leadership posts, and is now sharing with you the secrets to success.

Full of new tips and suggestions, this clear guide is comprehensive and thorough; it gives specific advice that makes you take a fresh look at how to prepare your interview and then face the panel.

Interview for a teaching job is the essential handbook that will give you insider information about all the stages of shortlisting, interviewing, decision-making before that all-important telephone call with the good news.

It shows you how to prepare so that you can perform well and demonstrate to the panel that you are the right choice for appointment.